Smarter than Jill

Smarter than Jill

95 true animal stories
You'll wonder what this cow is thinking

Avocado Press
Wellington, New Zealand

Published by:
Avocado Press
PO Box 22003
Wellington
New Zealand
www.avocadopress.com

Cover design: Simon Cosgrove
Typesetting: Dominic Hurley
Set in: Berthold Garamond
Cover photograph: Jenny Campbell
Proof-reading and typing: Vicki Andrews
Prepress: Megalith
Printer: Printlink
Accounting software: Fastbase Development Company
Compiler: Jenny Campbell
Unattributed passages are by Jenny Campbell

Printed in New Zealand
First published 2003, reprinted twice 2003
Copyright © 2003 Avocado Press Limited
ISBN 0-473-09415-0

All rights reserved. This book may not be reproduced in whole or in part, nor may any part of this book be reproduced, stored in a retrieval system, or transmitted in any form or by any means, electronic or mechanical, including photocopying, without written permission from the publisher, except for the inclusion of brief passages in a review. The views expressed in this book are not necessarily those of the SPCA or Avocado Press.

Contents

Introduction	vii
Foreword	ix
Acknowledgements	xi
1 Smart animals solve problems	1
2 Smart animals think of their tummies	9
3 Smart animals in mourning	23
4 Smart animals make us wonder	39
5 Smart animals speak up	59
6 Smart animals offer assistance	71
7 Smart animals learn fast	89
8 Smart animals go for help	109
9 Smart animals show cunning and have fun	119
Afterword	129
Future books you can be involved in	131
Submit an animal question	133
Submit a smart animal story	135
We'd like to hear your ideas	137
How to get more smart animal books	139

Introduction

Animals are fascinating, especially when they catch us out with their seemingly intelligent antics. Perhaps you've known a cat who used his Jellimeat to bait some fish or were amazed by sheep that took turns babysitting their lambs.

In this book you'll read about these and many other experiences with smart animals. You'll start to wonder what's really going on inside their heads. There are stories about horses, mice, seagulls, pigs, parrots, rabbits, sparrows, spiders, donkeys, dogs, cats, chooks, crocodiles, cows, bees, alpacas, mynah birds, magpies, crows, sheep, goats, a tiger, a robin, a weka, a hedgehog, a rat and a kea.

Smarter than Jack was the first book in the smart animal series. Published in September 2002, it became a best-seller and raised over $43,000 for the Royal New Zealand SPCA. It was a very fulfilling book to create and many people benefited from it.

In this book we've taken into account the feedback from readers of *Smarter than Jack*. As a result we've included more pictures and more stories and removed the chapter introductions.

The future of the smart animal series holds a number of exciting books. This includes an entertaining and informative book of quirky, humorous and obscure questions and answers about animal-related issues. We're also always looking for more stories about smart animals. See the back of the book for more details on how you could be involved or visit www.smarterthanjack.com.

This year we are publishing *Smarter than Jack* in Australia too. It will contain stories about animals such as bandicoots, wombats and kangaroos, and it's sure to make an engaging read.

We hope you enjoy *Smarter than Jill*. A good portion of the profit generated from book sales will benefit the SPCA.

Foreword

I've never been good around animals and birds. And I might add that some animals and birds have not behaved well around me.

I was a postie in Porirua long before dog attacks became widely reported. In those dim old days (around the time of the 'Wahine storm'), posties had to deliver court summons and fines and get them signed by the happy recipient. Many had dogs to deter us from our duties! I never flinched. If a dog came for me, I threw the mail away and bit myself in the arm as a warning to the dog.

Of course, this is a happy book in which animals do lovely, kind and interesting things. You will feel good reading this book and you will live longer as a result. Research shows that bonding with animals lengthens your life. If you are my unnamed radio colleague, you also live with rabbit droppings in the shag pile. But hey, you can't have an enormously long life which doesn't smell!

But why are animals so cute and clever? Some would say, too clever, many of them. The Japanese have invented a device which enables the owners to decipher dog barks. Do you really want to know what your dog thinks of you? (Soon it will be translators for sheep, goats and, worse still, goldfish. Goldfish see a lot of things around the house which ought not to be spoken of. Remember, through the fishbowl, we are their TV!)

These stories make you come over all warm and fuzzy. They will help you to realise, if you do not already, that animals like and admire us. They would quite like to be us!

Which is a comfort. At a time of international tension, the numbing loss of the America's Cup and GST returns, it is nice to know that Pungu the cat will steal bread for arthritic Jade the Labrador or that a goat will cooperate to move obstacles from the path of a motorist.

Smarter than Jill

These animals are showing willing, and they set an example of unconditional love and cooperation.

If the world's leaders were lambs, or cats even – well, the world would be a different place. If we lived simpler lives based on eating and sleeping (oh, that's right, I do . . .) and lacked ambition, pride and ego, we could all have a place in the sun.

Ah but even animals have problems, which is why we have the SPCA. But most of the problems are created by humans.

Strange that.

Gary McCormick

Acknowledgements

This book really belongs to everyone who has known or read about a smart animal. I find it strange putting my name on the cover, because so many others have had a hand in its creation.

This includes everyone who submitted a story, and especially those who had a story selected, as this provided the content for this book. The people who gave us constructive feedback from *Smarter than Jack* and participated in focus groups helped us make this book even better.

Peter Mason and the team at the SPCA were again keen to be involved. They assisted us greatly.

Anton my partner gave me continued support, especially when I gave up my full-time job in April to focus on publishing.

Gary McCormick wrote the fabulous foreword, Simon Cosgrove designed the cover, Vicki Andrews typed the stories and did the proof-reading and Dominic Hurley did the typesetting.

Production partners Megalith and Printlink did a grand job of producing the book.

Addenda again represented the book to bookstores and the bookstores wanted to sell it. Their support is and has been critical. Creative HQ gave me a challenging and inspirational place to base my business and the residents offered great support and advice and were excellent critics for my often obscure ideas.

Lastly, I cannot forget my endearing companion, Ford the cat. Although I must admit to feeling slightly disappointed with his seeming lack of intelligence that became increasingly evident as I read the many stories about smart cats. Perhaps one day soon he'll do something that will totally surprise me.

1

Smart animals solve problems

A lineup of lambs in the back paddock

Lamb care centre

One week I noticed each morning when I was leaving for work our six lambs would be all together in the driveway. They were in the care of two of the ewes while the other ewes were over on the grass stuffing their faces. Nothing unusual in that really, except I observed that each day there were two different ewes with them – they seemed to be working a lamb-minding roster as they all took a turn while the others were free to graze. After they had all taken a turn, the first ones came back on duty and worked through the roster again.

How did they know who was on duty? Who organised this system? It just goes to show that sheep are not really stupid at all. Not kindergarten but lambergarten.

We have one young ewe who used to leap about like a springbok when she was a lamb and now I see that her lamb is just the same. She stood staring at me for a moment, then took off leaping with her front legs tucked against her chest as she sprang forward. It really looks quite hilarious.

With such a small flock of sheep we have come to know them each as individuals and it really is quite enlightening to realise that sheep are just like any other living creature with their likes and dislikes, their friends and enemies, and their individual characteristics and habits that are not so obvious when farming large flocks of several hundred sheep.

Adrian Holloway
Palmerston North

One helpful goat

We share our long driveway with our neighbours. They decided to get a goat to help keep the driveway grass down, and so Steve (named after Steve Irwin) arrived.

He is a lovely animal who is also so considerate at getting up and moving away whenever a car comes down the driveway. He has a hut and a bucket of water that is moved with him up and down the driveway, and sometimes he even gets an extra bucket full of goat goodies.

One morning as my husband Frank was on the way to work in the ute he saw Steve sitting in the middle of the drive next to his bucket of yummy treats. Frank was thinking he would have to stop and get out to move the bucket as he wouldn't be able to manoeuvre past. Steve was also summing up, as he looked first at the ute, then back at the bucket, then back at the ute, then back at the bucket. He must have been coming to the same conclusion as Frank because, to my husband's amazement, Steve picked up the bucket and moved it over to the side.

Frank couldn't help but chuckle to himself as he drove past, but what really got him laughing was when he looked in the rear vision mirror to see Steve walking out to the middle of the drive with the bucket. As Frank watched, Steve put the bucket down in just the same spot as before.

Julie Aerts
Tokoroa

The baby snatcher

Missy was broody, she wanted nothing more than babies of her own. Here she was, a young fit German shepherd in the prime of her life and her owners had made it impossible for her to breed.

Not to be outdone, she went scouting around the neighbourhood for unattended little ones. At first her new babies were kittens carried home gently in her mouth to her kennel where she would proceed to contentedly groom them. Of course her embarrassed owners would then have to ask around the neighbours as to where to find the original mother so the snaffled ones could be safely returned.

Later she graduated to puppies and yet again the hunt was on so they could be reinstated in their original homes.

Thwarted she was not, as one day I looked out the dining room window and there was Missy guiding with her nose a real live human baby just at the toddling stage. Gently she was nudging him down the long drive toward her kennel. Neither baby nor dog thought this particularly unusual, it was me that was about to have kittens. My dog the baby snatcher. I could just see the headlines. Duly the baby was returned to the original owner with no ill effects to the baby or myself.

Realising we had to do something to stop this aberrant behaviour – and fortunately we were about to shift towns – we legally acquired for her a real puppy to guide into adulthood which, thankfully, satisfied her completely.

Jeff Allan
Auckland

Here's your letter

Many years ago we had a black sheepdog Labrador cross named Rita.

An elderly friend was staying with us for a short holiday; she wrote some letters, then walked half a mile down the country road to put them in the postbox. On her return she sat down for afternoon tea; five minutes later Rita walked in and put a letter on her lap. It must have been dropped on the way to the box.

Jean Whitehouse
Auckland

I'll show you the way

I live in the country and one day noticed a goat wandering on the road below my place. A lady over the road had two or three goats on her property and I assumed one had got loose, so I phoned a neighbour to say that one of Bi's goats was roaming the street.

Went back up to see what it was doing and there was Bi's aged golden Labrador leading the goat up the road. As I watched they passed me and proceeded up the drive into the place from where I assumed the goat had strayed.

'How lovely,' I thought, 'leading your friend home.'

Now this is the part of the story that makes it amazing.

Bi had kept goats for years but one day one of them decided to eat a shrub which was in the middle of their paddock, rhododendron if I remember rightly – maybe not. This was the wrong thing to do as it poisoned the old fellow – end of goat.

So the word went round there was a vacancy in the paddock. The neighbour I'd phoned earlier, re the goat on the road, had a friend with just the animal that needed a good home. The goat was duly brought out and, on arrival, tethered to the vehicle while everyone had a cup of tea. Mustn't rush these things.

The goat broke free somehow, the old Labrador I would say just happened to be about at the time and the two met.

Did the dog say 'Are you coming to live with us?', did the goat answer 'Yes' and then was he told 'Well I'll show you the way'?

Was there any form of communication? Or did they both know 'something'?

I think this is a truly amazing, delightful and heart-warming happening.

Margaret Rooke
Mahurangi West

Greater love hath no cat

Among my loved animal companions were two Siamese cats: gentle, intelligent and affectionate. The older one, Jasper, was a real 'Dad' to his younger protégé, and Smoke showed fondness of his senior.

This tale is of the occasion when the neighbour's dog had my old boy baled up in a tree in great distress. Smoke rushed next door to the dog's owner, who was in his garden – 'wailing like a fire siren' according to our friend – and led him back to the scene of the disaster.

Dog was taken home and cat rescued, but it was a mutual source of wonderment that the young cat went straight to the right person who could solve the problem!

To this day I feel Smoke saved Jasper's life. He then did it a second time when he came to me crying frantically and took me to where my old boy lay stricken with a stroke. After treatment by the vet, Smoke stayed by his friend's side, licking him with a protecting paw around him, to bring him back to life.

They were inseparable and never seemed to be apart for two more years of devotion.

Greater love . . .

Glenys Waterhouse
Hamilton

Togetherness

This story showed me that our cat Oscar and dog Wally, who lived with us as extended family members, could work as a team when necessary despite treating each other with disdain the rest of the time.

It happened this particular day that a small mouse had found its way into our lounge room and both these pets just loved the challenge of cornering and defeating a poor little mouse. Our house was set up in such a way that just around the corner through the archway into the family room was a piano. With both animals in hot pursuit the mouse raced around the corner and under the piano to safety.

Not to be defeated, the pair stationed themselves one each end of the piano, Wally at the far end and Oscar at the lounge door end. And there they sat for the next ten minutes or so. The mouse was going nowhere and neither were they.

Then to my amazement, Oscar (you could almost see him hatching this plan) stepped back from the piano and around the corner into the lounge and waited. This left a clear escape for the mouse at one end and sure enough about ten seconds later it ran from under the piano around the corner straight into Oscar's waiting paws. It was just so cleverly done.

Of course Oscar claimed it as his and rushed outside with it while Wally still waited patiently at the other end of the piano – until we were able to cajole him into coming and seeing for himself that it was all over. But it was not all over for him and ten minutes later he was sitting outside with the dead mouse beside him looking as proud as punch. You could almost hear him saying *my turn now – after all, I did have a bit of a hand in this catch too.*

Sue Brown
Ngongotaha

The pigsty cat

We have a cat, semi-wild, which lives at our pigsty and thinks it's a pig.

Several years ago she caught a sparrow and followed me and the cows up the farm race. I followed her to the sties expecting to see her give the bird to her month-old kittens – as yet unsighted by us. But no, she gave the bird to a black sow and was rubbing against the sow's front legs.

Some months ago the same black sow brought out her ten one-week-old piglets, which had been born in some pampas grass. I walked to the sties to feed the pigs and the black sow followed me, leaving her babies in the middle of the path about 180 metres from the sties and in the opposite direction to the pampas grass. The piglets were going around and around in a small tight circle, not sure what to do or where to go. The sow and the cat walked from the sties back across to the piglets, stayed by them for a few seconds, then the sow walked back to the sties. The cat walked across to the pampas, with the piglets close behind her. They went the 100 metres or so and then into the bushes to safety.

Unbelievable though it sounds, the sow must have told her piglets to follow the cat and she must have told the cat to lead the piglets to the pampas.

Michael Jackson
Kaitaia

2

Smart animals think of their tummies

Arthur the kea asking for a sweet

I'll take two, thanks

New Zealand's highly intelligent, very inquisitive and entertaining alpine parrot, the kea, has had to put up with a lot over the last 150 years. Early settlers in the South Island high country introduced thousands upon thousands of woolly, four-legged tussock munchers into the keas' habitat to eat their food supplies.

When keas hit back by eating the fat reserves from a few sheep, farmers began shooting the parrots on sight and appealed for government help to wipe out these 'vicious sheep killers'. The government responded by putting a price on the heads of these birds. Hundreds were slaughtered. It wasn't till 1970 that they were given partial protection. Keas are now an officially protected symbol of our high country. Remaining keas tend to congregate around Southern Alps ski fields and tourist spots in anticipation of easy-to-find food.

Staff at the Arthur's Pass tearooms have all been clearly told to always close the outside storeroom doors. Those who forget have found on their return to the store a collection of brownish green parrots on the back lawn, each enjoying their individual slice of rye, wholemeal or mixed grain. Inside, several plastic bread bags pulled from crates, neatly split open and their contents spread about. The keas keep watch, for they know that sooner or later a door will be left open. They strike with speed and precision.

It was early last year when one of these ingenious birds decided on a change of diet. Val, a long-time member of the tearooms staff, named this entertaining character Arthur. Arthur realised that if he stood by the shop's front door, sooner or later an unwitting customer would hold the door open, letting him in. Shrieks and squawks would erupt, not from the bird, but from customers on seeing a parrot march into the shop.

An undignified scramble across the polished floor brought Arthur to a cane basket on the counter front. This was filled with small white paper bags labelled '50c mixture'. A quick shuffle of bags and he could grasp the corners of two in his beak. A hasty flapping retreat usually got him back out through the still open door. Returning to a side lawn, or the far footpath, this feathered raider then proceeded to tear a hole in the bottom of each bag, withdrawing and devouring the sweets one by one. Sometimes sharing them with others of his kind. If he had only managed to secure a single bag, or lost one during his exit, then as soon as this one was empty he'd return to the shopfront. He then proceeded to pace up and down outside the glass with a most impatient air, until the door was opened and he was able to acquire a second packet. Curiously, after consuming two packets he does not return for more.

They put up a sign warning customers to keep the sweet-beaked bird out, but few even read it. Putting the '50c mixtures' behind the counter resulted in Arthur changing to chocolate fish, but he makes a real mess with them. Filling the basket with cakes of chocolate resulted in several torn wrappers every time he attempted to take one. The '50c mixtures' are now back in the basket and the loss of $1 two or three times a week is regarded as a tax paid to the keas for the privilege of doing business in their territory.

Neville Guthrie
Timaru

A resourceful cat

Smudge was a black and white stray tabby cat that adopted me when I flatted in Mt Wellington. He was one of a family of feral cats that lived on a vacant section behind the block of flats that I lived in.

Although Smudge lived rough and generally shunned human contact he seemed to like me and would come and say hello whenever I hung out my washing. I started feeding him and slowly over time he became more and more friendly until he would often come inside my flat and sit on my lap.

Even though I fed Smudge every day his instinct was to hunt. He would stalk birds but I never saw him catch one. He did however catch rats and mice which he would leave on my back doorstep as if he thought he was giving me a gift.

Then one day he took up a new sport.

I was inside when I saw Smudge hanging around the goldfish pond in the tiny garden in front of my flat. From where I was standing it looked as if he had something in his mouth. I crept up to the window and watched him. He put his face down to the pond and appeared to drop something into the water though it didn't look like a goldfish. As I watched, Smudge just sat there poised, intently looking into the pond.

Soon I saw the surface of the pond ripple as goldfish came to the surface. Smudge's paw shot out and into the water, making a small splash. His paw returned empty-handed. I rushed outside to shoo him away from the pond. When I got there I saw the most amazing thing. A blob of Smudge's Jellimeat was floating on the surface of the pond, which the goldfish were hungrily nibbling at. Smudge had gone fishing and had used some of his dinner as bait!

For the next couple of weeks he tried this trick almost every day until I finally put some chicken wire over the pond to keep him out.

Alexandra Day
Auckland

The best solution

A funny story about our fox terrier Cuthbert who will do anything for a ride in the car.

One evening he was eating dinner when my daughter Annika was off out in the car and 'invited' Cuthbert to come.

Caught between his love of food and riding in the car, he picked his bowl of food up (obviously spilling some) and took it with him!

Linda Flounders
Remuera, Auckland

Fishing for chips

The fries were greasy, and the birds were hungry. As we sat overlooking the Kapiti Coast, we were entertained by a raucous, squabbling group of seagulls. Strangely, the most successful member of the gang was not the fattest, or the loudest, or even the meanest bird.

We noticed him because he perched on the railing above the rest of the group, refusing to be involved in the scavenging and fighting so obviously beneath him. This alone was enough to tempt us to throw a chip or two in his direction. But he surprised us.

Whoosh! He flew into the air, and snapped the chip up in his beak, catching it before it had the chance to hit the ground. Impressed with his abilities, we threw him another. *Whoosh!* Keen to impress again he leapt up, catching the chip on the full and gobbling it down. We threw him another, and another, amazed at his tricks, and trying to catch him out, until we'd nearly used up all our chips, and even a bit of burger.

But it wasn't over yet. His finale involved swooping into a full loop before catching a chip in his beak, moments before it hit the ground, and flying just overhead of the other seagulls. He seemed to be showing off, saying 'Ha ha, look, I got the last chip. I'm cleverer and much more charming than you!'

He was certainly a character and made our lunch that much more enjoyable. He was definitely the smartest seagull we have ever come across.

Louise Studholme and Kate Benton
Wellington

Donald the pony

When I was five years old my father gave me an Iceland pony. He was lovely; he had a very thick coat and it felt like sitting on a cosy rug and my little legs were stretched to the limit.

We all loved Donald dearly and my mother decided that he was very intelligent. She would teach him some tricks; for instance, he had a water bucket in his pony paddock and mother taught him to pick it up in his mouth and bring it to the gate for a refill. For doing this he got a treat – he loved bread.

Now and then he was put into the front paddock. There were large double gates into the garden and it didn't take him long to learn how to lift the iron latch on the front gate and come into the garden, usually at night, for a nibble of grass and a few tasty flowers.

We had a long, wide veranda the full length of the house and early one morning my parents were woken up by the sound of hooves thumping along the veranda and a pony's head bumping the glass door of their bedroom, I suppose for one of mother's treats. He was scolded and put back in his paddock. They thought someone must have left the gate open, their daughter perhaps!

However a few days later mother was horrified when she went into the kitchen to see Donald standing in the pantry with potato juice dripping from his mouth and bread etc all over the pantry floor.

Our lovely clever Donald had not only opened the gate, but had opened the back door by pulling the old-fashioned latch with his teeth, pressing it down and then pushing it forward. Quite a simple procedure for an intelligent animal after all.

Now all he had to do was to go up a few steps into the pantry, remove the lids from several pottery crocks that had knobs on the top and help himself to a wonderful feast.

I remember he had to be backed out, but he didn't fuss. I suppose he thought, 'Oh well, I'll find something else later!'

He was a wonderful child's pony; we had him for many years. He was 18, maybe older, when we finally said goodbye to our tricky old friend. I have never forgotten him and that all happened a long time ago.

Moire Hepworth
Auckland

Too many birds spoil the flavour

Being a couple of city workers, our ideal getaway place was a deserted beach. We found one north of Colville on the Coromandel Peninsula. Far from the crowds we set the billy to boil and lay back in the shade on a crimson blanket of pohutukawa flowers.

No cars, no cellphones, no other beings – wait – there was one, a quietly watchful red-billed gull.

We tossed him a crust of bread. The gull snatched it up, turned and scurried down the shell-bank. He then sauntered across 15 metres of sand, dropped the crust in the tide and waited for the next incoming wave. It returned his bread, salted and moistened, to his feet. Having savoured the morsel the bird strutted back up the beach, over the shells and stoically stared at us.

A solitary seagull is a fascination to those of us used to flocks of skirling gulls squabbling over litter in city playgrounds. So we offered the lone gull another crust, which he again took the time to carry down to the tide for seasoning.

When he next came up the beach, a companion gull flew in. We threw them each some bread and they toddled off together to process it in the sea before eating.

Only one more bird joined us for lunch but when it did there was an immediate change in behaviour. The new imperative was to gulp

Smarter than Jill

A bird on the lookout

down on the spot whatever was for the taking. 'Salt and water with your bread?' Not likely. Their preference for a little relish with their food was quickly forgotten in the company of competitors.

That day three gulls on the Coromandel coast presented a charming illustration of how one is opportunity, two is company, three is a crowd, and crowds definitely spoil the quality of life.

C Mackinder
Waitakere City

The patient robin

Years ago, when we were tramping at the Nelson Lakes we met three women on the track who told us that we would see a robin waiting for us.

We were sceptical, but sure enough there was one sitting on a log beside the track. He hopped up when he saw us coming. I put a small piece of sultana on the log and he hopped over and ate it. Then he flew up and sat on my pack for a few seconds as if to say thank you. He then flew and settled on the log, ignoring us, obviously waiting for his next arrivals.

> Molly Green
> Taupo

Wily weka

A few years ago I was camping in the Abel Tasman National Park during a beautiful Nelson summer. I woke early and opened the front of the tent to enjoy the ocean view.

It was then that I saw the weka, just outside the tent. To my surprise, it was removing the pot scrub and all the cutlery (about six pieces) from the unwashed billy, eating the mashed potato off each fork and off the sides of the pot. It then proceeded to go around the corner of the tent and take the tea towel off the top of the billy containing the water boiled for breakfast . . . and washed its face in it before wandering off to the next tent.

Pretty clever bird that weka.

> Karen Malone
> Nelson

Perfect pears

Our neighbour's sheep grazed in a paddock containing a pear tree. At the sound of a pear falling to the ground they would rush from wherever they were to eat the ripe pear.

While the 'winner' ate, the remainder would look hopefully up at the tree. The sheep would then position themselves to be the first for the next pear and keep an eye out for where their 'competitors' were.

Beth Muir
Dargaville

Hedgehog's brunch

The morning was hot and still. A hen was cackling in the fowl yard beyond the sparse hedge of the next-door section.

A movement under a shrub attracted the observer's attention. Out ambled a half-grown hedgehog who looked around and then snuffled towards the hedge. It seemed to be searching for something. Just what became obvious when the hedgehog squeezed its way through a smallish hole in the wire netting and wandered into the fowl run.

Several minutes later the animal reappeared pushing an egg with its snout. Carefully and without hurry, the egg was guided through the hole, and was closely followed by the hedgehog.

Slowly the egg was rolled across the lawn until it came to a raised concrete path leading to a clothes line. Instead of going round the edge of the path, the hedgehog used its snout and two front feet to lift the egg the two inches required to get it on the concrete. Quickly scrambling onto the path itself, it very gently moved the egg to the edge and somehow lowered it back onto the lawn without damaging the shell.

More nudging and pushing with its nose, the animal, with the egg, arrived at another path, which bordered the section on the other side. The lifting procedure was repeated and the egg was pushed under the house.

A tapping noise followed and the watcher investigated. The hedgehog was bumping the egg against a house pile. Success at last, when a hole appeared in the shell. Hedgehog's tongue ensured that not a drop of the contents was lost.

Judging by the numerous empty eggshells in the vicinity, the venture was not a first attempt.

Was the hen's cackle the dinner gong?

Joan Edwards
Allentree

A gift of cherry stones

Living where we do with so many trees, we always have the pleasure of seeing mother birds with their young during the spring, so this year it was fascinating to watch a mother blackbird trying to keep her three 'always' hungry babies happy.

It was also a worrying time for my husband and me as we are owned by five cats. Two are too fat and lazy to even try and catch their own shadows, one has never been known to catch anything other than a butterfly, the remaining two I am afraid are villains!

When feeding our own 'boys' we also gave the dear old boy from next door a small meal. Scotty by name, he had been visiting us twice a day now for a long time and was always fed outside the front door. One morning he left a few Proplan biscuits and I noticed the Mother Blackbird was collecting them to feed her young. I wondered whether or not these would be good for the little ones, but I trusted her judgement; she after all was a good mother and wouldn't feed her young on anything which was liable to harm them.

So each morning the same ritual, Mother would wait for Scotty to move off and then she would clean up. I put a water bowl under a tree for them, as I knew that when eating this dry food, water was a necessary item.

We noticed lots of cherry stones being left on the front steps. It could only be the birds, but why, it had never happened before and anyway the cherry tree is in another part of the garden well away from the frontage. Then one afternoon I had the front door open. I was preparing to feed our 'boys' when in hopped 'Mother' and dropped a cherry stone on the mat. I knew then, this was her gift to us for the biscuits.

'Mother' still visits to drink or have a bath in the bowl. One offspring is here most days, the other two visit on the odd occasion.

Kath Pickett
Taranaki

Seagull savvy

Seagulls have to have a certain amount of street savvy in order to survive. We have, however, encountered one that may be smarter than the rest.

Having disembarked the Interislander at Picton, we decided to fortify ourselves with hot chips before driving south. As we sat on the sand where we could watch the comings and goings of the harbour, we were soon joined by the usual scavenging gulls. Annoyed by their unwanted company, we decided to play a trick. Our chips were piping hot – too hot for even a greedy gull we thought – so we threw one to the nearest bird and laughed when he inevitably dropped it.

Imagine our amazement when he then picked it up again and, holding it gingerly in his beak, scooted down to the water's edge, dunked the chip and, having cooled it, ate it, and then came back for more! Not being able to quite believe what we had just witnessed, we threw him another chip and were treated to a rerun.

Cheryl Phipps
Auckland

3

Smart animals in mourning

Bovine bereavement

This is an account of the reaction of our small herd of Jersey cattle to the death of a calf. It involves Merlin the bull and the three cows, Bonnie, Betsy and Pixie.

Pixie had calved almost eight weeks prior to this event, but her calf was not very bright and could not find his mother's teats (hence his name, Sim, as in Dim Sim). He was suckling up around her flanks and so did not receive the colostrum milk that is so essential for a calf's early development and prevention of illness.

It was too late when we realised what was happening, but by this stage the damage was done and he required extensive veterinary treatment and constant attention from us to nurse him back to being able to feed himself. He had even been blinded temporarily by infection and spent most of his time simply sitting or lying in the paddock with his mother.

For the next six weeks, once he was over the worst of his disabilities, he showed little improvement. He was still very unsteady on his feet and walked as though he had severe arthritis. He still spent most of his time sitting down and only struggled to his feet to feed, after which he would totter about in much the same place for about quarter of an hour before sitting down again.

Smarter than Jill

Pixie the cow

Then one morning I was milking Bonnie in the cowshed and saw Pixie up on the hill standing on her own. I would normally expect to see her feeding Sim at this time and wondered to myself where he was.

When I finished milking, I moved the rest of the stock into another paddock and Pixie, who was isolated with her calf, came down to the gate by the compound. Thinking that perhaps she wanted to be given a little more of the centre race that had thick, lush grass that we had been break-feeding to her to supplement the rather dwindling feed in her own paddock, I opened up the race to her.

Pixie walked in and stood there looking back up the hill to where I had seen her standing when I was milking, gave a moo, then turned around and returned to her old paddock. As she passed through the gate she paused and looked back at me with a look that indicated that she wanted me to follow her. As I did so, she broke into a trot, heading straight back up the hill. When we reached the top of the hill, I saw to my dismay what had been bothering her; Sim lay flat out on the ground, cold and stiff.

Pixie stood over him and, after sniffing at him briefly, gave several long mournful cries. It really sounded pitiful. Deep shuddering bellows.

I left her there to mourn while I returned to the house to fetch a spade. When my wife Gemma and I returned, the other stock had gathered at the compound by the cowshed, sensing something was amiss. As the reason for Pixie's confinement no longer existed, I decided to let the others in to join her.

We all returned to the hill to where Pixie stood over her prostrate calf and as we arrived she turned to greet us. She stood there as her own surrogate mother, Bonnie, tried to rouse Sim, licking his muzzle, blowing in his mouth and lifting his head with her muzzle.

Merlin stood off a little way, then bellowed at us to move so that he could approach Sim as well (he is a little wary of us and does not like us to get too close to him), so we moved away and let him approach the dead calf also. He sniffed at Sim, then put his face up to Pixie's and gave her a very gentle nudge with a little grunt that came across as a communication of condolence. He then moved away to the front boundary fence and bellowed loudly for some time. Was he perhaps announcing to the other herds in the district that we had a bereavement?

We left them gathered around the site for a while, then returned to dig the grave close by. All the time we were digging the grave, Pixie stood over her dead calf and Merlin continued to bellow at the boundary fence. We lowered the body into the grave and Pixie watched us bury him. Afterwards she stood there and started to bellow once again; a long loud moo, followed by an intense shuddering sob as she drew her breath back in. A sound not unlike a donkey braying. She spent the rest of the day and most of the next standing or sitting by the grave-side, still mourning the loss of the calf that she had had with her for the past eight weeks.

Now some people think cattle are just dumb animals that do not have feelings or communicate as we do. The conclusions we draw from this experience are quite the opposite and confirm our belief that they do indeed feel emotions that are common to us humans and indeed, I suspect, to most animals.

Other studies have shown that monkeys and elephants behave in a similar way when a member of their group dies or loses an infant, but in our intensive commercial farming of cattle, it would not be easy to notice such behaviour.

Several other incidents over the past few years of dealing with such a small herd of cattle have shown that they are no different to any other living creature. Likes, dislikes, friendships, happiness, sadness and so on are not exclusive to humans but also can be found in most other animals if one has the time and opportunity to observe them.

Adrian Holloway
Palmerston North

Mark of respect

Almost six years ago, the agonising decision was made to end our lovely sheltie's life. He was 17 and a half years of age and had bladder cancer.

The telephone call had been made for our local vet to come out to our property to undertake this very sad deed. Laddie was such a loyal friend who had given us so much love during his lifetime. It was very sad to know that his life was soon to come to an end and we knew that we would miss him terribly.

When the vet came, we noticed our donkeys looking at us through the fence most intently, wondering what was happening.

Just after dear Laddie had died, my husband said I should take a look at the donkeys. The four of them – mum, dad and their two daughters – were standing very close together with each head bowed over another's neck. They held this position for quite a while. I have never seen them act like this, either before or since Laddie's death.

I am sure they knew he had died and that was their way of showing their respect. It was certainly very special to see.

Brenda Wollen
Upper Moutere, Nelson

Trixie – her last goodbye

I was sitting on the back steps enjoying a mug of coffee in the early spring sunshine when I became aware of someone or something trying to capture my attention. It was Trixie, our ancient 16-human-years-old grey tabby cat. Poor old Trixie was a rather plain old puss with no apparent redeeming features other than her constant affection.

Smarter than Jill

Trixie the cat

    She was just sitting on the wet concrete path staring at me as if in a trance. I looked into her tired old yellow eyes and she just stared back without a blink as if willing me to pick her up. It was all rather surreal. I felt obliged to talk to her and she responded by making a painful effort to get onto my lap. I duly patted and cuddled her, thinking

'How bony you are Trix'. She relaxed on my lap for a wee while. I gave her a kiss on the head and with as strong an effort as she could muster up, she very purposefully left my lap and headed for the shed with a strength that I had not witnessed for some time.

I had a foreboding about her behaviour; so I went to investigate why the almost sprightly walk to the shed. And there she was, on an old rug, quite dead.

She had obviously sensed her time on earth was at a close. Needless to say, I shed quite a few tears at the shock of finding her within minutes of being in my company.

On reflection, I feel quite humbled that she chose to spend her last moments on my lap as a final parting.

We miss you Trix.

June Spragg
Auckland

Our corgi and the Jersey bull

It was about 1974 and we were farm workers in the district of Manawaru near Te Aroha.

A Jersey bull on the farm became cast; he had his hind legs paralysed. It was near the house.

We went with our corgi dog Lindy to see if we could get this animal up – to stand. We pushed and pulled. 'Speak up Lindy' we asked, that means she can bark. They have quite a yap, a piercing bark. The bull was concerned and alert – yes, he was trying, but none of us were able to entice him onto his feet, so we left him in peace.

Next day we mowed some lawn, gathered a little hay and a bucket of water and took it to the bull. He was shy and would not eat in front of us for a couple of days, but eventually he became less concerned.

Each day Lindy would accompany us as we took fresh food and water, then turned him to another side. Lindy would talk to the bull and make these noises in her throat like *ium ium ium*, then she would lick his face. The bull got quite used to us, though we were not making any progress.

Then came the day the boss rang Wallace Industries. The 'dead' truck arrived, the driver got out with a gun. My small children and I were watching from inside the house. Lindy, not quite a year old, was on the chain; she was barking furiously. Next thing she was off, she broke the collar, she had that man bailed up. I had to scamper across the paddock as fast as I could. Took her back to the house; by this time the children were frantic.

Then we heard that horrible blast of the gun. The children cried, and that little dog howled and howled. She whined and pined for a good week over that bull.

What amazes me to this day is she had never seen a gun before or an animal die. Yet by golly she knew.

Grace Scott
Matamata

A caring goodbye

We have had kune-kune pigs for a number of years and have always found them to be real characters. We enjoy their company and love them all.

One kune-kune of note is Katy Pig. A large elderly sow, she is a bit of a bossy boots with young pigs, but great company for boars when they are not 'on duty'. Consequently she and Piggles, our first pig, spent quite a bit of time together in the tree gully beside Whistle

Alley. Call one and they would both come running, so it was a bit of a mystery when one day we couldn't find old Piggles.

I looked right along the gully to no avail. My mother-in-law checked too, but still no sign of Piggles. Piggles wasn't the sort of pig who pokes through fences, but we checked with the men in case they had seen him somewhere he wasn't meant to be. Had they shifted him? No. I started searching the paddocks in widening circles away from the gully. I even walked up and down the railway line, looking for a corpse and checked the most likely of the neighbour's paddocks. No luck anywhere. It was starting to look as if someone had taken our pig, though we couldn't believe anyone would, as he was elderly and would not have made good eating. He did have a great set of tusks, which may have been a prize for someone, but surely they wouldn't have taken the whole pig if that was all they were after?

The mystery was solved about a fortnight later, when my father-in-law returned from a tree-planting expedition in the pigs' gully. He reported that Piggles *was* still in the gully where he had been put, but was no more, having died peacefully. The reason that none of us found him was that Katy had carefully and lovingly buried him. He was lying in a little hollow above the side of the creek. Katy had built a nest around and over him, covering him so well that I had passed by within two feet and never spotted him. Indeed, if the wind hadn't blown a little of the grass away from his snout, affording my father-in-law a glimpse of a tusk, we would have been none the wiser.

We were touched and intrigued – burying deceased herd members is something that elephants do, but none of us had heard of this behaviour in pigs. It wasn't just a one-off either, as not long after this we pig-sat an elderly boar called Percy. Percy's mate had died not long before we got him, leaving him a sad and lonely pig. When his people returned from their OE they decided he looked so happy with Katy that they couldn't bear to split them up and so he stayed on with us.

Percy died one night the following winter during a snowstorm and – you guessed it – Katy began to bury him too.

Unfortunately for Katy, we have run out of elderly husbands for her at present!

Ngaire Taylor
South Otago

In mourning too

My father was taken with a terrible accident in 1959. Our Jersey cow had only been milked by dad.

The day of the accident, that cow stood with her head over the gate at the house, with big tears running down her face and landing on the path. She had never been there before, usually she was as far away from the house as she could go!

That was a sight I'll never forget. That night, a man tried to milk her, nothing! A lady neighbour came, and talked to her, and she let her milk down.

It's funny, mum and I never thought much of her before that, just a cow! She remained one of the family, till her end.

Gloria Herrick
Tuatapere, Southland

A doggy wake

When my mother was a teenager, she went to stay on a remote farm in the King Country with her Auntie Annie Grice. During the time she was there, word came through that a brother of her aunt's had died suddenly while at a stock sale.

Findlay McDougall had lived alone on another remote farm in the Upper Retaruke district. The undertakers took him to the mortuary and later to another town to be buried so he never returned to his farm. As he was a single man of 45 years, a neighbour looked after his stock until some decision could be made as to his estate.

About a week after his death my mother and her aunt travelled to his farm to deal with his clothes and goods inside his house. My mother was asked to take her Uncle Findlay's clothes from the house and hang them on the clothes line to air. These were clothes that had been in the house all along.

Findlay's four dogs, which were having the freedom of a run loose from the chain at the time, immediately went and sat under the clothes hanging over the line and began to howl. My mother said the sound was so eerie and heart-wrenching that after an hour or two her Aunt Annie and she could stand it no longer and removed the clothes back inside. Immediately the dogs stopped their howling and went voluntarily back to their kennels.

How could those dogs have known their master was dead and given him the equivalent of a doggy send-off?

Celia Geary
Manawatu

A fitting goodbye

Barking and growling menacingly, Toby, a red miniature dachshund, greeted Oscar, a timid four-month-old rough collie puppy. As the eldest pet, Toby was head of the household and it was only with many cuddles and a good number of dog biscuits that he finally rather grudgingly accepted Oscar into the family.

Smarter than Jill

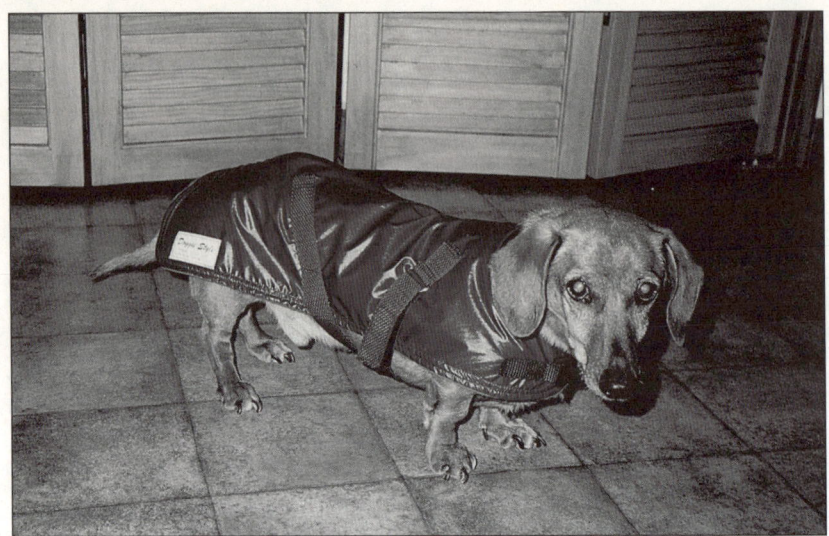

Toby in his new coat

Oscar and Toby did become friends although the age difference meant that Toby rarely joined in boisterous play. Their favourite adventure was to bark enthusiastically at a possum in the pear tree who calmly stared down at them from the branch.

Three years later, at nearly 16, Toby spent most of his day stretched out in the sun or curled up in his pullover-lined box, a former wooden kitchen drawer. Toby still loved food however and would eagerly sit under the table or near the bench, ready to lap up any falling stray crumbs. As winter approached, a friend made him a navy blue, red-lined dog coat to wear on the cooler winter nights.

Then one tragic day, Toby uncharacteristically wandered onto the drive and was killed by a backing car. That night as we said goodbye, Oscar slowly wagged his tail and gently sniffed Toby. He was buried beneath a lavender bush. It was an emotional evening as we all recalled Toby's many years with us and our three children.

Smarter than Jill

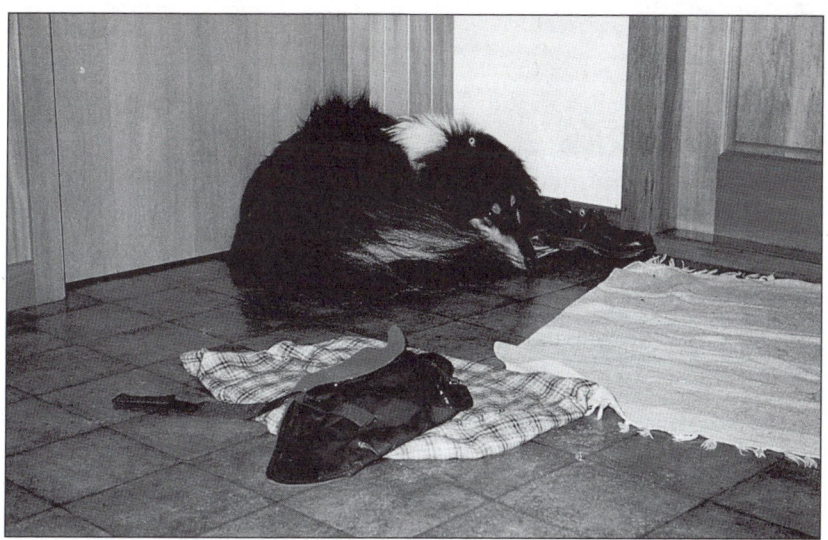

Oscar and Toby's coat the next morning

Early the following morning I walked into the kitchen where the two dogs slept. I was astonished to see Toby's navy dog coat lying on Oscar's cushion with Oscar stretched out on the floor nearby. During the night, he had taken Toby's dog coat from the closet where it was kept and placed it on his cushion. Then he went back to sleep. Perhaps this was his way of saying goodbye to Toby as he never did this again.

Several months passed and it was Oscar's turn to greet the new arrival, an exuberant sable two-month-old rough collie called Teddy. Still playful two years later, Teddy gets placid, laid-back Oscar running and chasing over the hills with him.

Marcia Ringle
Little River, Banks Peninsula

Charlotte's Sapphire

Charlotte was about ten years old when her love for horses emerged. As time went on her desire for horses grew and she began to have riding lessons. While taking lessons at the Country Club Riding Academy in Johnsonville, Wellington, Charlotte discovered that a number of girls were 'working' on Saturdays in return for some free riding lessons.

The thought of spending one whole day with the horses really excited Charlotte and we commenced the weekly trek to Johnsonville so that she could have her wish.

Having completed a year of this we decided that her love of horses was not a passing phase and one of the instructors helped us look for a suitable horse.

This was how Sapphire joined the family . . . a beautiful white horse with a wonderful nature. However Sapphire was not perfect, she had been involved in an accident while being transported on a truck that was not equipped to carry horses and had badly damaged one eye. Fortunately, the instructor knew Sapphire and was certain that Sapphire would be a perfect horse for Charlotte. So against the vet's advice we bought her.

Charlotte had a lot of fun with Sapphire, taking her to pony club and winning many ribbons but most of all just enjoying each other's company. As a parent it was wonderful to know that Charlotte had a horse that you could trust.

As time went by, Sapphire's eye became more of a problem and a melanoma developed. We kept a close eye on it but eventually there was a danger of the tumour eroding a large blood vessel. After much soul-searching and time passing we made the heart-wrenching decision to have her put down.

It was a dreadful day. By this time Charlotte was right in the middle of sixth form exams and of course none of us wanted this to happen.

We met the vet in a paddock next to the one where Sapphire was kept and Charlotte went to get her beloved pony while sister Melissa and the rest of us waited in silence.

It was one of those moments that you wished would go away: did this really need to happen, perhaps it wasn't as bad as we thought it was. Please someone do something so that this does not need to happen.

I happened to glance back at the paddock where Sapphire's paddock mates were. The three horses had formed a circle with their heads together in the centre close to the ground. They were just standing there very still. It is a sight I will never forget.

Ann Rose
Lower Hutt

4

Smart animals make us wonder

Becky the cat

Becky's gift

Becky is a very friendly grey ex-SPCA cat who has lived with me for nine years.

Among the regular gifts from the garden, one night at 2 am, via the cat door, she brought a young rat. By the time she woke me it was dead so I put them both back in the garden to play! Next morning, no sign of the rat so I presumed Becky had had an early breakfast.

However, three days later at the picture framers 14 kilometres away, I was aware of a strange smell from my handbag. Back home – Horror, as I emptied my bag on the kitchen floor. I think Becky knew and I vowed never to leave an open handbag on the floor again.

Diana L Stewart
Meadowbank, Auckland

Knowing Zac

About six years ago I told my dog Zac that I wanted to be with him when he died. He must have understood and remembered what I said.

On the day Zac died I'd bundled him up in the car to drive him to my parents house. I had organised for the vet to come round to their house in the early evening to put him to sleep. As Zac and I left home I told him that he didn't need to hold on for me, that I would be okay and if he didn't want the vet to put him to sleep and wanted to die naturally.

When we got to my parents, I collected Zac's stuff from the car, made a bed for him in the house and set a few things up to make him comfortable. When I finished bringing everything in I went back out to the car to bring Zac inside. When I got to the car Zac had moved and was sitting between the front and back seats. I quickly went to go and help move him, and as soon as I had him in my arms he passed.

Zac died in my arms; he had waited for me to come out of the house so that I could be with him when he died. I believe that he remembered what I asked of him years ago and that he listened to me earlier that day. He decided that he wanted to be with me when he died and to die naturally.

Susanne McNair
Hamilton

Crafty bee

Towards the end of the summer of 1992/93 our nights were suddenly disturbed by an intrepid bumblebee that came blundering through the bedroom window one afternoon and got caught against the glass.

Fran found him and fished him carefully out with a piece of card, only to find herself repeating the procedure five minutes later; and then again five minutes later than that. Bemused and at a loss, she blocked the window with the net curtain thinking the problem resolved.

But the bee was not to be outwitted so easily and she was called back to the bedroom when a fierce row broke out to discover him enmeshed in the folds of the curtain.

Out he went again and the window jammed shut on a sultry day, which finished the business. Or so she thought, until she ran into him in the hallway, on her way out of the bedroom. He came motoring through the open front door having found his way round to the front porch in the time it had taken her to close the window. He was self-absorbed and purposeful in that distant preoccupied manner of the working bee, showing neither fear nor favour, while giving Fran the uncanny impression that he knew exactly where he wanted to go. But she was having none of it and shepherded the recalcitrant bee back out the door, then closed it and returned to the sunroom.

It took the disgruntled insect five minutes to locate the open door at the back of the house, then sail gaily over the chair in which she was sitting, down the passageway and back into the bedroom. Intrigued now, she shadowed him into the room, where he did a couple of loops in his blundering bumblebee way before landing on the top of the wardrobe.

The peculiar aerodynamic design of the bumblebee seems to deny them the ability to steer in a straight line. He had a couple of clumsy attempts at landing as he swung round the room, divining a course through the principles of apian guesswork, which he seemed to use his memory to improve on. Then cast a final perilous loop over the bed to grapple a foothold in a pile of sleeping bags, narrowly missing getting caught in the dangling lampshade in the process.

This was the start of a two-week stay that settled into a regular routine.

Crafty, as our son Kas was quick to christen him, would sleep out the night, before waking about dawn with an ominous rattle. Then he would crawl from the sleeping bags, launch himself, then career off towards the window. If he had not made it into the outside world by the fourth attempt, one of us would climb blearily from bed to help shake him out of the curtain.

Often he would be back within an hour, kipping down again until nine, when he would cruise off for the day, returning for another short kip at four o'clock before heading out to work a twilight shift. Then he would return at dusk for the night.

His short stay brought with it all the anxieties attendant on looking after small children. He would wake in the night to flop prematurely off the wardrobe, then lie growling under the bed until retrieved back into his sleeping bags. On one occasion he fell behind the wardrobe itself to conduct a stand-off with a large and rather terrified spider, while I tried to shoulder the wardrobe out from the wall and rescue him.

Finally, desperate for uninterrupted sleep, we tried interring him in a shoebox at two o'clock one morning as he began revving round the room like a wind-up blowfly. He registered such violent disapproval at being shut up in this way that we resigned ourselves to our fate and left him to go on his merry, disruptive way.

Our feelings ran the gamut from parental resentment to sentimental affection and engaging curiosity at finding ourselves host to such an absurdly overconfident and somewhat surly guest, though such feelings were always qualified, for we knew he might be gone at any time, without explanation. This event we awaited with a sense of resignation as the fate of all such animal encounters. When it came, however, after a fortnight's occupancy, his leaving upstaged anything we might have imagined.

He missed one night, but then flew back in the open lounge window the next afternoon, something he had never done before. He then circled the room three or four times as we sat in our chairs, before flying back out the same window.

He was gone for good, though two days later we located him in the front garden, lapping up nectar from flowers in the lavender bush. At least we imagined it to be Crafty, for how can you tell one bumblebee from another save through guesswork. Our guess, however, was shrewdly informed by the fact that he now had a companion, and the two were working in obvious concert, as they milked the blue flowering bush.

Derek Schulz
Whanganui

Recruiting rats

Opening the back door one evening to feed the cats I was confronted by a startling sight. There, sitting side by side, looking at me with wide eyes, was our female cat Lucky – and an enormous rat!

It didn't appear to be hurt or bleeding and I think they were both so exhausted they had decided to call a truce.

Now, a mouse wouldn't have worried me – in fact I think they're quite cute. A rat dead or alive is another matter. I utterly abhor them. Mo, our other, smaller cat, was crouched on the steps looking terrified and I knew just how he felt.

I slammed the door shut and pounded up the passage to my son's bedroom shrieking, 'a rat, a rat, there's a bloody big rat out there!' He dropped the phone and left his girlfriend dangling on the other end. (It was a toll call too.) I woke my husband with the commotion but I didn't care. I was absolutely freaked out.

My son got rid of the rodent promptly, and also had to feed the cats that night. I wasn't going to venture out there again.

I still shudder when I recall what happened and I open the door very carefully to feed the cats now. So far Lucky hasn't repeated her trick.

That same weekend there was a novel fundraiser at one of the local hotels – Rat Racing. Was she bringing recruits for it I wonder?

Margaret Fearn
Nelson

A curious instinct

I grew up in South Africa and studied nature conservation. This interest in wildlife led me to working extensively with reptiles. I gave lectures on snakebite treatment, and due to my interest and ability to remove problem snakes, crocodiles and other reptiles I was often requested to do so.

For two years I researched Nile crocodile behaviour and noted a few interesting things during this time.

One was that crocodiles could predict cold weather. When cold weather was approaching, a crocodile would not eat – as if by some mysterious means it knew that it would not be able to digest its food. This often amazed our friends when we could tell what the weather would do – before it was announced on television!

Often with heavy rains crocodiles would move to higher ground when lying on riverbanks instead of moving into the water, why we would not know. Perhaps the water became too muddy or too cold.

These observations regarding behaviour were reinforced one evening three years ago, when I was called out to remove a 'problem' crocodile. The crocodile had travelled a few kilometres away from the river and had decided to lie in the culvert of a fairly busy road. This road runs from Pretoria to Mozambique and passes through the town of Nelspruit in the Mpumalanga Province of South Africa.

On arrival we were greeted by a sea of anxious faces and members of the police and fire brigade as surprised as we were at this 2.3-metre crocodile. After a few minutes of struggling we managed to capture the crocodile and take it home. The idea was to check for any injuries and then release it the following morning.

On the way home we discussed our surprise at having found the reptile so far from water and that it had even crossed a busy road to reach higher ground. As there was no drought at that time of the year – the rivers were full, and we actually had had a lot of rain during the week – we had no explanation. Why would a reptile that felt safe and secure in water leave safety?

The next morning we released the crocodile downriver, thinking we had done a good deed in returning it to its natural habitat.

That night the skies opened with a vengeance. It rained and rained and rained.

We then suddenly understood why the crocodile had moved to higher safer ground. Eventually Mozambique flooded and emergency help had to be called in. America even sent food and blankets, and major rescue operations took place.

Geraldine Pieterse
Warkworth

Fraidy cat

Three years ago our family acquired our first cat in four years. We called her Lulu, and she was a tabby. Even though she is now a full-grown cat, a bit of a timid kitten still remains in her. Since we moved to our new home, Lulu has been trying to mark her territory against two *very* bossy cats next door. Having failed this (being small and timid), she now rarely ventures outside.

Then one day, Lulu followed my Dad outside, as she feels safer out with human company. She scampered up a big pohutukawa tree outside our house. A moment later my Dad heard a squawking noise coming from high up in the tree. He thought to himself 'Lulu must be upsetting some birds'. But a second later Lulu dashed from the tree and bolted to the house, closely followed by two screeching birds! We laughed at it, but poor Lulu! She'll go down in history as the cat chased by birds!

Cassie Richards
Wellington

George

George was one smart little dog!

The tiny Yorkshire terrier was found in South Auckland as a pathetic little lost dog. The pads of his feet were worn from weeks of roaming, and his coat was matted and dirty from lack of shelter from the elements.

Our SPCA hospital staff observed that his teeth were rotten from obvious neglect and that, although an adult dog, he was still 'entire'. We performed both operations (teeth extraction and de-sexing) in one black Friday, at the end of which poor George didn't know which end hurt the most!

Being soft of heart I took him home for the weekend to recover, and when it was time to bring him back to the Animal Village for adoption he objected by going on a hunger strike which lasted for four days. In sheer exasperation the staff asked me to take him home again to see if he would break his fasting and eat . . . And eat he did, the moment his tiny feet hit our kitchen floor.

George had won with his little act of rebellion and for the next seven years he became my ultimate companion, accompanying me wherever I went – to work, on holiday, to the ivory towers of big business, to meetings, on community and school talks, on very public occasions where we often jointly appeared on television together – George was never far from my side. He also shared with me moments of deep sorrow including the loss of my dear wife from cancer, when he provided that comfort, companionship and understanding that animals do so well.

And in the end, when I had to make that final decision for him, I held him close to me, and he gave me that grateful and forgiving look before he took his last breath and slipped away into his final peaceful sleep.

Yes, George was a smart little dog because he captured a great chunk of my heart.

Bob Kerridge
Chief Executive
SPCA Auckland

Attitude!

According to the NZ Miniature Horse Association's temporary certificate of registration, Petite Cheval Mis-Chief is a one-year-old chestnut pinto mare with a white blaze. To us she is just Missy, a beautiful, whitish over-weight miniature horse with a brown tail and a white and brown striped face.

Our Missy has attitude! When we called on the breeders and put our names down for a foal, we noticed this little horse that was almost always on her own, despite several other mares running happily together in nearby paddocks. I suspect it was this attitude that prompted the breeders to offer her to us. We were novices with a couple of acres in town who were tired of mowing the lawns. What did we know?

Missy was safely delivered into her newly created paddock. The grass was lush and she happily grazed among the clover and buttercups. We tried to bond with her by offering food. She ignored our calls. I'd sit in the paddock reading a book, hoping she'd approach me. She kept her distance. I noticed that horse poo was starting to build up and foul the paddock so decided to start mucking out.

Armed with gumboots, a spade and a light blue bucket, each day I went into the paddock and collected the largest lumps of poo. Missy began to follow me, occasionally pushing over the bucket with her nose or strategically placing her front hoof in the bucket so I couldn't add to its contents. One day, she followed me to the gate. I slipped the catch, squeezed through the opening with my filled bucket and closed the gate behind me. As I went to walk away, Missy called out to me. When I turned, she put her head down into the grass, picked up a dry lump of poo and placed it carefully on the fence railing. I guess I'd missed some!

Missy has developed into the most loving best friend that we could wish for. Even the 'real horseman' who lives across the road from us admits that she has a beautiful nature. But our Missy still has attitude!

Alison Sutherland
Masterton

A sense of unease

It is over 80 years ago now since I had the following experience: an experience which seems even more vivid and wonderful as the years go by.

In July 1921 I was living in La Paz, Bolivia with my husband, little son and an Airedale terrier, Binkie. I had been in South America for three years and, as I suspected, I was going to have another baby. I was due for a vacation so it was decided that I should go home to England and 'kill two birds with one stone'.

In November 1921 I sailed for England, taking my son with me, but leaving my husband and the dog behind. I can see Binkie's eyes now as I said 'goodbye' to him, so sad and full of reproach at my seeming desertion.

I arrived in Liverpool in due course, where I was met by my parents. It was lovely to see them again, and to present my son, whom they had not previously seen. We travelled by train to London where my parents lived, and I stayed with them until it was time for my confinement. In April 1922 I entered a nursing home and on April 30 gave birth to a little girl.

A few nights later something happened which has caused me to marvel on many occasions.

The matron had left me, leaving a night light burning on my bedside table. I drifted off into a delightful sleep – when – suddenly I was wide awake. I slowly and reluctantly opened my eyes, and there, beside the bed, perfectly defined in the dimly lit room, stood Binkie. At first I thought 'How did he get here?' Then letting my common sense control my imaginings, 'It cannot be his physical body, that is quite impossible, it must be his spirit.'

Tentatively I put out my hand to pat him and I was not surprised, having heard this is the way ghosts behave, that my hand just passed through him! Binkie looked at me with love in his eyes, and as I returned his gaze, I noticed that the hair on his chest was damp and matted together. I could not understand this at all, but as I was trying to reason it out, he quietly and unhurriedly faded from my sight.

The following afternoon my mother came to see me, and I told her all about my extraordinary experience, but being very practical all she said was 'You must have been dreaming, the result of an overactive brain'. This remark left me wondering whether it was a dream or not, I just did not know what to think about it at all.

That same night, when the matron had taken the baby from me, and left the night light burning as usual, I turned over and prepared to go to sleep. However, it was not long before I had an uneasy feeling that someone or something was watching me. I turned round, and there standing beside me, exactly as on the previous night, was Binkie. I again tried to pat him but my hand just went through him as before. I then found myself saying 'Good old Binkie, what do you want?' My voice seemed to disturb the vibrations because shortly after I spoke he faded away. Though I felt sad at his departure I realised in some miraculous way he had managed to contact me, in spite of the miles of land and sea that separated us.

The next night the vision repeated itself in exactly the same guise as before, but that was his last appearance. I never saw Binkie in ghostly form again.

Now for the sequel. About four weeks after my nocturnal adventure, I had a letter from my husband. Letters took approximately a month to come by sea from South America to England as there was no airmail in those days. In this letter, after giving me all his personal news, he told me that Binkie had been very ill with pneumonia. In fact no one thought he would survive. My husband tended him night and day, after following the vet's advice to put mustard plasters on his chest to relieve the congestion. I realised then why, when I saw Binkie standing by my bedside, I had noticed the hair on his chest as a damp, tangled mess.

It seemed so wonderful that the dog, through the bond of love and understanding that existed between us, had managed to show himself to me as he appeared during his time of sickness. 'Indeed truth is certainly stranger than fiction.'

Time passed, and my husband wrote to tell me that Binkie had recovered. I was overjoyed of course, and when the time came for me to return to Bolivia I was looking forward tremendously to seeing him again. Thus we were reunited and were never very far from each other, until he passed peacefully away some three years later.

Valerie Ross
Dipton

Moa's determination

I work at a pre-school with children from two to five years. In October 2001 one of the staff brought in a new class pet. This was a young cockatiel. She had been chosen as she was born with a birth defect to her wings, which meant she would never fly. So her owners removed her from the aviary because she was being picked on by other birds. They thought she might do better in a cage. I decided to call her Moa after the extinct flightless bird.

When I first met Moa she looked like a little pompom, a ball of feathers hunched at the bottom of her cage. Moa's disability meant she had limited balance. We put a very low perch in her cage, only to see her nosedive into the bottom of her cage when she fell off it. Moa spent most of her days at the bottom of her cage walking around and peering out at the world she could see from her low position. She had an interest in the world around her and began to experiment on ways to see the world.

I watched as Moa developed a system for getting around her cage by using her beak and feet. By coordinating beak and feet she could pull herself up and along the bars. She would use beak and feet to hold onto her cage while she looked out onto the world. Unfortunately this system almost led her to disaster.

One day I noticed she had been in the same position for a long time. On closer inspection I noticed she had one of her tiny toes caught in a bar. I managed to free her and she seemed all right. At the end of the day I went to check on her and found her huddled on the floor of her cage in a small pool of blood. I mended her foot and took her home not expecting her to live. I put her cage next to that of my other birds and covered her and kept her warm. Moa survived and regained her strength. I decided she would be happier at home living next to other birds.

Moa decided not to repeat her method of travelling around her cage and instead practised climbing the new ladder I had bought her. Using beak and feet she climbed up first to the bottom-most rung where she held on tight with her beak. She fell off once or twice but persevered, climbing higher and higher.

I got a shock one day when I looked low in her cage and did not see her. I lifted my eyes higher until I saw her clinging to the very top rung of her ladder, proudly looking over at her next-door neighbour. But Moa didn't stop there. Tiring of constantly holding onto her ladder she practised balancing on her perch. She'd move forward and back trying to find a way to stay on her perch. Eventually she stood straight and proud on her perch only about ten centimetres off the ground. But she didn't settle for her low perch. As she increased in confidence and agility she got bolder, standing on higher perches. If she fell off she would just use feet and beak to climb up again.

Eventually, several months after I got Moa, she stood without falling on her topmost perch and looked down at the other birds below. Moa was finally king of the castle!

These days Moa is a different bird to the one that scuttled around the bottom of her cage. Although she will never fly and also has eyesight problems she is still a hero and a clever girl in my eyes. She overcame all her disabilities and was determined not to spend her life at the bottom of her cage.

That's my story of my bird Moa. I'm rather fond of my girl as she has achieved so much for a bird with her problems.

Maree Mascard
Helensville

Paddy the Wanderer

Paddy the Wanderer was a prominent and much loved figure on Wellington's wharves in the 1930s. He was well cared for by watersiders, seamen, taxi drivers and many others, becoming a waterfront identity, till his death in July 1939.

He was believed to be the pet of little Elsie Marion Glasgow who frequently went with her dog, then called Dash, to meet her seaman father when his ship returned to port. When Elsie died of tuberculosis aged just three and a half, it is believed that Dash, bewildered and bereft, took off to the wharves and looked for her for the rest of his life.

So the legend of Paddy the Wanderer was born. The friendly Irish terrier (or part thereof) embarked on sea voyages whenever the spirit moved him. He travelled extensively throughout the 1930s, visiting many New Zealand coastal towns by boat, but always returning to home base – No 1 shed at Queens Wharf. He also frequently rode with the local cabbies.

Paddy was known for his street manners. He would only cross the road on a green signal. He was a dog that nobody 'owned'. Even when he fell ill and the cabbies tried to settle him in their homes, he wouldn't have a bar of it and promptly returned to his residence of choice.

On his death in 1939, notices were placed in the *Evening Post* and he was placed in a coffin, which carried the words 'Paddy the Wanderer at rest'. A funeral cortège of 12 taxis carried his body to the city corporation yards in Chaffers Street for cremation.

Paddy is remembered with a memorial plaque and drinking fountain on the Wharf apartment building opposite the entrance to the Museum of Wellington City & Sea on Queens Wharf.

Jennifer Campbell
Wellington

A sixth sense?

When I was in England I lived with my mother and five cocker spaniels. Four of these dogs were as fond of me as they were of Mum. The eldest dog, Major, was very much a one man's dog, as Mum got him for company while I was away from home and Major only saw me at weekends.

When I lived permanently at home and we got the other dogs, Major continued to look on me as second best.

One day Mum went to Plymouth to visit a friend. It was an hour's bus journey from home. I stayed home with the dogs.

Major was very upset and ignored me. He wouldn't eat and just moped. At about 3.30 pm he suddenly perked up and no longer ignored me – everything was normal again.

I told Mum when she got home and she said that she got on the bus to come home at 3.30 pm. How did Major know that? Mum had not done that trip before while she had Major. It has always intrigued me.

Joan Meyer
West Otago

A whirlwind of vultures

During my expatriate years in Botswana (heart of the Kalahari Desert) I was fortunate enough to work on a wild game reserve. Naturally most of my time was taken up by creatures of the four-legged variety, but luckily I was also able to spend much of my time observing the prodigious variety of bird life. I had previously believed that to be called a 'bird brain' was unkind. I left Botswana with exactly the opposite belief!

The reserve owner had created a 'Vulture Restaurant' on the reserve. Although we had no permanent residential vultures on the property, the popularity of the restaurant had spread to the two vulture colonies, which were both within a 50-kilometre radius of the reserve.

The food for the Vulture Restaurant was supplied compliments of the local abattoirs who were only too pleased to get rid of the enormous amounts of abattoir wastage. Every Friday afternoon leading up to the weekend slowdown, the white utility vehicle from the abattoirs would trundle into the reserve and would head for the Vulture Restaurant to offload its cargo.

This weekly procedure worked like clockwork – the food would arrive just in time to be offloaded by 4 pm, which gave the abattoir workers half an hour to get back to the abattoir to knock off for the weekend.

It was what would happen every Friday afternoon before the abattoir vehicle's arrival that I learned to wait for in amazement. At around 3 pm winter or summer, an enormous whirlwind of vultures would arrive and continue to build up in the skies above the reserve. The very air would appear to be alive with the movement of hundreds of pairs of wings lazily surfing the currents, the living whirlwind growing larger and blacker as the minutes ticked by and more and more of these voracious giants joined in the ever growing circles that marked the eye of the whirlwind.

Around half an hour after the initial build-up of these birds, the eye of the whirlwind would begin to reach lower and lower until with a great screeching and squawking the trees and ground surrounding the Vulture Restaurant would come alive with the arguing giants and the fluttering of their wings would become almost deafening. And then the silence would fall, equally deafening – until, yes, the sounds of an approaching vehicle could be heard in the far distance. The meal was arriving.

Quite often when I recall the awesome sight of a vulture whirlwind I ask myself whether they were able to recognise their meal on wheels from the air, and if so, how did they know to look for it on mid Friday afternoons? Instinct or intelligence – what is the answer?

Wendy Roberts
Lower Hutt

One determined chook

I well remember growing up on a farm in central Taranaki. Animals always played a big part in our lives. Cows, geese, pigs, dogs, cats and even a pet eel called Peter. All were special and loved.

However, it was the chooks that have made a lasting impression on me. They were all colours and running free, which made hunting for eggs very time consuming and difficult. There were plenty of good hiding places, evidenced when fluffy chickens appeared at feeding time. Now, none of these chooks had names but all had their own personalities.

One chook in particular was a very good layer and her favourite place to lay her egg was not under the big barberry hedge but on the tractor seat parked in the shed.

There was many a day when Dad was using the tractor on the farm. Our chookie always seemed to find it, sometimes running and cackling, other times flying in spurts to meet the tractor, finally perching on Dad's shoulder. It was as if she was saying, *I need that tractor back in the shed to lay my egg.* Some days she was more desperate than others and that all-important egg would be laid on Dad's lap.

Joan Dickson
Te Awamutu

Suddenly lowered to the level of the insect world

What then? One might get wings, perhaps like a bee, or a wasp with a tiny waist, the way it used to be fashionable for ladies, such a slender waist and with generous curves, maybe with golden and dark stripes too.

Such a one came buzzing around me while pausing for a sit-down on the grass and some refreshment. It was during a long walk over the hills up Pipiriki way in full sun and the Wanganui River down below sparkled under it. I waved the buzzing thing away.

A friend sitting there, a keen bee-keeper, glanced up and said nothing. The thing was buzzing back anyway and trying to land upon the hand that held the glass. Again I waved it away.

'That bee is probably thirsty,' commented the bee-keeper.

Was it a bee then? Bees and wasps always looked much the same to me, with the possibility of difference as between a sunny day and a wet one. Thirsty? I had never thought that of bees, but what did I know about them except that they make honey and, oh yes, wax too.

This one hovered close with some determination. I kept still, glass in hand, hand over knee, to see what would happen. She circled ever closer and came back once more to land undisturbed on the rim of the glass, already less than half full. She poised there for a short moment like measuring a distance, dived in, surfaced, shook her wings, stood balanced upon the liquid surface head down, wings beating for a few moments, flew out and away. A complacent smile played on the lips of the bee-keeper gazing after her.

I looked doubtfully at what was left of the drink. Cold it was . . . a bee, the friend had said, a young one . . . well, after all, I eat honey . . . so I finished the drink that the young bee had bathed in and shared with me. Thinking how pleasant the sight of water is, how good cool water feels on a hot day and what a big, deep, inviting pool half a glassful of juice would look to me if I were the size of a bee.

I Rozani
Wanganui

5

Smart animals speak up

Cindy the dog

Cindy, loyal to the last

Cindy was our first puppy, a $5 mutt. She was rejected by her owners when they discovered the expensive, arranged mating of her pedigree corgi mother took place after her shameless, secret night of passion with the disreputable beagle/something up the street. I bought the six-week-old scrap to comfort my young children – and me – after my husband's sudden death, and on that very first night of rapturous cuddles I quietly broke for good my first house rule: no sleeping on beds.

Cindy never won a prize at dog obedience classes or a beauty contest. Her only clever trick was her habit of positioning herself against the dangling foot of anyone seated with knees crossed, and mesmerising the owner into non-stop chest rubs. But what Cindy lacked in brainpower, she more than made up for in heart-stealing affection and character, and we utterly adored her. My mother, with a lifelong distrust and distaste of dogs, once said as she stroked Cindy snoring on the bed beside her breakfast tray: 'I've never liked dogs, but there's something special about Cindy.' Then, at the end of her long life, Cindy saved mine.

At almost 14, she was dying of cancer. Heartbroken, I took leave from work her last few days, placing her basket, now that she could no longer spring onto my bed, close to it each night so that I could quickly attend to her. One night, woken by a whimper, I leaned over and stroked her. The whimper grew urgent, and I rolled over to switch on the light before getting up. And saw, silhouetted against the starry sky, the terrifying dark figure of a man, already halfway through my large window, one knee already on the sill as he prepared to climb over it. My scream frightened Cindy, but also startled the man who shot backwards, and fell off the picnic table he'd dragged there before fleeing into the night.

After the police had finished their cups of tea and left, I was still too shocked for sleep and sat cradling my dog for mutual comfort till dawn. Next day, yielding to urgings from concerned friends and professional advice, I drove Cindy to the vet's for the last time. My anguish at losing a beloved mate was intensified by one agonising thought: Cindy probably saved my life, and I had taken hers. Then a friend showed me some words from another grieving owner.

'It broke my heart when I had to have him put to sleep. Later it dawned on me that what the vet said was right. Probably the kindest thing I ever did for my best friend was the very last – and the hardest. I released him from his pain and let him go.'

Twenty years and two more much loved SPCA waifs later, I still see that funny little face, eyes closed in ecstasy as she sways in time with the foot, every time I cross my knees – and smile.

Valerie W Smith
Belmont, Lower Hutt

Who needs a loudspeaker?

When my children were young, before New Zealand had a million people, the community was a lot safer for children to roam, playing where they will or visiting other children. Telephones were not common and when a child was wanted, one stood in the yard and called their name.

However, I had a little help with the locating of my children in the guise of the local mynah birds. When I called a child's name, one of the mynah birds also began calling the child and another down the street took up the cry and pretty soon the wanted child would turn up, saying that the mynah had told them they were wanted.

The icing on the cake was when one bird was on the ground and the other one sat on the fence watching out for it. When a cat started to stalk the one on the ground, the one on the fence would give the alarm. You would think the one on the ground would fly off to safety but no, it would turn to face the cat and say *Meow*. This would bring the cat to a very quick stop. It would sit up and peer at the bird in confusion and you could see the question going through its head, *Are you a cat? If you are, you are the strangest one I have seen*, and as with all cats, when in doubt, groom and so it did. The birds could then get on with their own business without any further molestation.

Lorraine Rodley
Whangarei

A birdbrain

Dim-witted people are sometimes referred to as birdbrains. What an insult . . . to birds.

Birds are smart. And none more so than parrots – as Chippy our grey cockatiel frequently demonstrated.

Chippy loved to exercise his linguistic skills. *Here we go*, he'd squawk as my husband Gavin lifted his cage from the stand for its weekly cleaning. *Here we are*, he'd announce as Gavin set the cage back in place.

The clever bird would add his voice to mine during the nightly ritual of herding our several cats outside. *Quick, quick, quick*, he'd yell as the felines dithered in the doorway.

But not all of what Chippy had to say would have passed muster in polite company. Like children, parrots have an uncanny ability to latch on to naughty words.

I will never forget the evening I arrived home from work to be greeted, not with the usual *hello, boy*, but something altogether ruder. *Hello, little bugger!* Chippy shouted.

Scarcely believing my ears I asked him to repeat what he had said. *Bugger!* screeched Chippy.

Where had he heard the word? Certainly not from me. And certainly not from television. This was before the Toyota ad gave the expletive a degree of acceptability.

Eventually we worked it out. Caged birds are messy creatures. They perform their natural functions indiscriminately and they fling seeds in all directions.

'What a dirty little bugger you are,' Gavin would say in affectionate exasperation as he scrubbed Chippy's perches. His comment had evidently hit home. From then on 'bugger' became a regular part of the cockatiel's vocabulary. And he used it to telling effect.

For most of his time with us Chippy had had a budgie companion, Squeak. When Squeak died we decided to provide a lookalike replacement. Thus Bugsie joined the household. While a lot feistier than his predecessor, he was otherwise virtually Squeak's double.

How would Chippy react? Would he cotton on to the fact that this was a different bird?

Of course he would! There was no fooling the intelligent cockatiel. Chippy sidestepped along his perch and, putting his head on one side, fixed the noisy newcomer in the adjacent cage with a beady eye. Then he hopped onto his ladder and examined Bugsie from a different angle.

Chippy spent the rest of the day looking – and saying nothing. He seemed to be trying to make up his mind about the budgie.

At length he delivered his verdict. It was exactly what we expected.

Little bugger, Chippy said.

Jenny Lynch
Lynfield, Auckland

We should have listened

This story is about how Wally, our spaniel cross dog, taught me a lesson that I won't forget in a hurry.

It was the day before the cattle sale and our ten cattle had been put in the house paddock ready for an easy round-up the next morning and a short walk to the neighbour's loading ramp. We lived on a small lifestyle block that was close to the city boundary and my greatest fear was that one day the cattle would escape and get into city properties causing havoc and property damage.

My husband Keith and son had been working hard around our front boundary that day and were happy to relax in front of the tele that night. Just after dark Wally had gone outside as he usually did but this night he started barking incessantly. This was not altogether unusual for him as he often bailed a possum up a tree with the same response. We ignored him for a while but then he appeared at the door. Keith told him it was okay – he could chase his possum. On the third appearance at the door and much more barking we thought we'd better check out what he was up to. He led us out the front drive and began to head down the road towards the city. We told him not to be silly – everything was okay and to come inside – which he begrudgingly did.

The next morning I was up early to get the cattle to the yard and to my horror – no cattle. The gate had been left open and the cattle were gone. My worst nightmare had occurred. But luck was with us. The cattle had turned left at the end of our road instead of going straight ahead into the city. They had taken the longer route to the main highway, and just the house before they hit the highway one of our neighbours had been arriving home late, saw them all over the road and had put them in his holding paddock for the night.

We often grazed the cattle outside the front of the house when grass was scarce so how did Wally know they weren't just grazing that night? He knew something was wrong and tried in vain to tell us.

We never again ignored his actions.

Sue Brown
Ngongotaha

Phone home

We gave a baby budgie to our daughter Denise for her tenth birthday in 1961. Because he was a beautiful shade of green we gave him the Irish name of Paddy Murphy.

In no time at all Paddy learnt to talk and would say things such as *My name is Paddy Murphy and I must not play with sparrows, ring 81827 please, pretty boy, where's Denise?* and *Gidday mate, how would you be?*

We let Paddy fly around the house at night and didn't ever trim his wings. Once he got out and flew away. He landed on a lady's shoulder. He had flown across the Waikato River and was several miles from our home.

Paddy began to talk after the lady walked home. He said *ring 81827 please*. She rang us and asked if we were the Murphys and if we had lost a budgie called Paddy Murphy. We were overjoyed to get him back.

Paddy was a real little character with heaps of personality and he loved company. We remember him with fond affection.

Kath Haliday
Hamilton

A wow wow wow in the nick of time

For the last few years I have frequented an old bach in a remote part of the Coromandel very close to the beach, separated from it only by a few sand dunes. It was on one of these occasions two years ago that the following event took place.

My four-legged friends are two completely different toy dogs: Cindy a 14-year-old miniature pincher (a sleek black and tan beauty in her day) now totally deaf with impaired vision struggling to maintain dominance over the household pet population, and Gemma a ten-year-old griffon who resembles a sandy-coloured shaggy floor mop of quiet nature.

The bach back door was slightly open as the humidity was high that morning and I was relaxing on the couch reading a novel. The dogs never wandered outside without me. *Wow Wow Wow*. Gemma was standing directly in front of me, her huge brown bulbous eyes focused. *Wow Wow Wow*. I ignored her. With little jumps forward she barked again, *Wow Wow Wow*. I'd only ever heard her voice a few times – most out of character.

Thinking perhaps someone was nearby I checked the door. Something was wrong, where was Cindy? A thorough search of the rooms with Gemma barking at my heels revealed she was missing. Panic set in, she had never wandered away before. In desperation I ran outside to scan the hillside, now oblivious to Gemma's relentless barking. *Wow Wow Wow*. She followed me, as I scrambled to the top of the sand dunes to survey the beach, not believing that her little arthritic legs could carry her that far. There, to my absolute horror, I could see a small black figure way down on the beach walking in circles close to the incoming tide.

I ran like never before in my life, plucking her from the wet sand to comfort her, guilt sweeping over me for not having been more vigilant. Trembling in my arms she was fearful and confused, I could see it in her eyes. Gemma stood silent on the crest of the dunes. She followed me back to the bach with a little wag of her tail, the barking had ceased.

Cindy made a full recovery from her ordeal and Gemma resumed her quiet disposition. I learnt a valuable lesson that day. They had communication way beyond what I would ever have anticipated. What a tragic end it could have been had it not been for little Gemma and her *Wow Wow Wow*.

Gail Armitage
Avondale, Auckland

Letting her thoughts be known

Josie the cat always sat on the right-hand side of the sofa when she was inside. When we got a television it was on a little table next to the right-hand side of the sofa.

Josie did not like that 'thing', it made a noise. One evening she jumped onto the TV, looked down over the edge, extended a paw and smacked the newsreader smartly on the face.

Sarah Mills
Feilding

A mother's orders

While living in Tonga a few years ago, I witnessed an incident with a hen and her one-day-old chicks.

The hen was moving around on a grassy area, her chickens milling around her as she pecked at the ground.

A dog rushed at them, took one of the chicks in its mouth and ran underneath a building to devour the mouthful. The hen made a sound that caused all the other chickens to scatter and hide in different places in nearby gardens while she, making loud distress noises, ran towards where the dog had disappeared ... She continued making alternate sounds of distress and the different sound which I could only assume was a keep-out-of-sight sound to her chicks until the dog came out from under the building and slunk away as she rushed at it.

After the dog was out of sight, she made another sound, and her chickens, from their different hiding places, came running back to their mother.

Cynthia Green
Whangaparaoa

Musical bunny

My Toffee is a bunny with personality plus. A perfectly beautiful Lop-Ear Dutch Miniature, he lives indoors, is toilet-trained and is an endless source of delight and amusement.

He has what is surely an unusual rabbit habit. He is very choosy about the music he likes. I teach singing and he sleeps soundly under a bed until the first student arrives, when he shoots out like a rocket, dances around them as a welcome and settles down to listen. However, his taste in voices varies and sometimes he disdainfully departs to another room!

The most humorous incident for me was when some practice for myself was indicated. He bolted out like lightning to investigate this new singer and his consternation when he couldn't find the person in the usual place at the end of the room was really hilarious. After bob-tailing it into every corner, he finally spotted 'the old girl' behind the piano. Registering horror and disapproval he thumped his feet and took off to the farthest corner of the house! Alas I got the message that my performance was greatly inferior to that of my pupils!

Glenys Waterhouse
Hamilton

Help, we're dying of thirst!

I bought four young hens from a battery farm. They became very tame and attached to me.

I dug over a section of the run every day or two and they scuffed through the soil looking for insects and sprouted grains of wheat.

One morning, in the hottest period of summer, I was digging the run and the hen that would jump onto my shoulder came over to me and began to peck quite hard on the side of my left leg. Peck, peck, peck, peck, on and on.

'What are you doing Gawky?' I said, and she immediately went over to the water container and tapped and tapped with her beak. *Tap, tap, tap, tap, tap.* It was completely empty – I had left them without water for several days in the hot dry weather! So I filled it straight away and Gawky drank and drank and then the other hens all drank till the container was empty. I filled it up again.

Clever girl.

Adelia Finlay
Rotorua

6

Smart animals offer assistance

Cats Casey and Titch

An act of gratitude

Casey revealed a giving nature from early on. A fearless black and white cat, Casey was only a year old when I brought home a tiny black part-Siamese kitten and called him Titch.

Far from being jealous, Casey was forever showering little Titch with gifts from the garden: live mice, assorted plant material, grasshoppers and, much to my horror, fearsome-looking giant Wellington wetas. Ideal toys for a kitten to play with.

Several years later Titch became terribly ill. In pain, bloated and unable to move he was suffering from what was eventually diagnosed as a blocked urethra, which was to ultimately prove fatal. I made a bed up for him on the bathroom floor and was watching over him anxiously when Casey came in and gently licked him. Then he went out and returned holding a small ball of wool in his mouth. He dropped it on the floor near Titch's bed and, batting it gently with his paw, urged him to play. When Titch didn't react, Casey proceeded to bring him other play objects, including a wine bottle cork – he must have ransacked the kitchen tidy bin for this – until eventually there was a cluster of gifts on the floor.

I was totally amazed by this 'feline play therapy' behaviour. However, the ultimate of Casey's gift-bearing acts was still to come, and it happened like this. One afternoon Casey appeared with a wound above his shoulder. I concluded it was the result of a stab from a large beak – almost certainly inflicted on him by the young, cheeky magpie who spent time in our garden, and whom he often stalked.

As Casey had licked the wound clean, and as there was no sign of bleeding or inflammation, apart from saying 'It serves you right', I dismissed it . . . that is, until the next day, when I saw with alarm that a huge abscess had formed. It was Sunday. Casey was in distress. What was I to do? I reached for my trusty manual on cat ailments and soon had the answer.

For about 15 minutes or so, Casey was the perfect patient as I repeatedly bathed the abscess with hot water to bring the pus to the surface. Then, voila, suddenly it erupted! I cleansed the site carefully and applied tea tree oil as my final ministration, after which, obviously much relieved, he lapped up a saucer of warm milk and disappeared outside.

Shortly afterwards I heard Casey meowing at the back door, which was unusual as there was a cat door. I went to investigate. On opening the door I saw he had vanished, but there on the top step was the most beautiful little nest! I couldn't believe my eyes. 'How did that get there?' I wondered. Then the penny dropped – Casey! In utter disbelief I picked it up. It felt as light as fairy-down – a beautifully woven construction of horsehair, fine grasses and moss, exquisitely adorned with tiny feathers, moss and lichen.

Perhaps it had been blown down in a recent storm, or perhaps he had fetched it for me from where it nestled in a tree. I still have this little nest and will always treasure it as the gift my clever cat chose for me.

Amazing but true.

Margaret Harold
Wanganui

Magpie heroes!

This summer I was pleased to discover a wild duck sitting on eggs in our gully paddock. Despite a tree being chopped down beside her (before we knew she was there), she managed to hatch out her ducklings and wandered down to the pond with them.

One day, while walking in the next paddock with the dogs, I heard the mother duck making an awful racket. When I looked over I saw her defending her babies from a hungry hawk. I was about to run over there to chase the hawk away, when a magpie came swooping down and chased the hawk away. The magpie then returned to the duck family and stood nearby watching the sky, as if on guard. The duck family returned to their swimming and seemed quite relaxed around the magpie.

Smarter than Jill

I have also seen magpies chase hawks away from our chooks. In defending their territory, they obviously defend what other creatures live in it too.

We have lots of native birds living here and, in the 13 years we've been here, have never seen the magpies chase them. We enjoy the magpies' singing and can't understand why so many people want them killed. We are very grateful that they choose to live here and hope that thoughtless people won't wipe them out completely. It would be a great loss of a very intelligent bird.

Mrs L D Pattison
Mamaku

The little dog

Owen Farnham, with his wife and family, owned a farm at One Tree Point until about 35 years ago when they moved to a farm at Waiharara, north of Kaitaia. They sold the farm and it was developed for housing. Part of it is now known as Paradise Point.

Between then and now, Owen reached the age of 85 and, hale and hearty, he retired to Kaitaia, with his son Charlie taking over the farm.

For many years Owen has driven himself out to the farm to help out. He catches and saddles his horse, unclips his two dogs and, with his grubber across his shoulder, puts a few sandwiches and a thermos in his backpack and a few other essentials in his pocket. He then rides off to inspect the place, grub a few thistles and jot down in a notebook anything that might need doing, such as fence repairs.

On one particular day he had ridden right out to Big Hill near the back of the farm and came to grief opening the gate while on his horse. The gate swung the wrong way and, in turning his horse to get the gate, the horse's rump touched the electric fence. The startled horse bolted, dislodging its passenger who lay on the ground with a broken femur. The two dogs snuggled down beside him while he pondered about a man he had heard of who survived in a similar predicament for three days before he was found.

It was not long before the next-door neighbour's little dog arrived on the scene. This little dog was not a frequent visitor to the farm; in fact Owen had never seen him out there before. He had a sudden thought that the little dog might go home to his owner, if Owen and the big dogs chased him off. First, Owen patted him and took out his notebook and wrote . . . 'I am out by the gate to Big Hill and I can't walk, Owen'.

Owen always carried rubber bands around his notebook, so he tucked the note around a couple of rubber bands and stretched the bands around the dog's neck. Owen then chased the little dog off, shouting 'Get home, get away home'. The big dogs joined in with loud barks. The little dog went away but he didn't go home.

Meanwhile Charlie had arrived back at the farmhouse and his wife said, 'I'm a bit worried about your Dad, he should be back by now.'

Charlie had just about set out to look for him when up trotted the little dog, tail wagging. When Charlie bent to pat him he noticed the note tucked in around the little dog's neck with rubber bands. He was so surprised to see the little dog because he never visited by himself, but sometimes came over with his owner, the next-door neighbour.

It wasn't long before Charlie and his wife were off in the four-wheel drive to find Owen back in the rough country. They brought him out carefully, phoning for the ambulance on the way via cellphone.

It didn't seem long before Owen was back on the horse again. He was amazed at what the little dog had done.

Joan Phillips
Ruakaka

A gift of bread

Our black Labrador Jade was in her later years and began showing signs of arthritis. We covered a cot mattress with a blanket and placed her 'bed' in the lounge where she was fully involved in family life.

It wasn't long after that I noticed slices of bread, some half-eaten, on and around her bed. Having three children aged from three to nine, I supposed it was one of them and chastised them for feeding her in the lounge. They all denied doing so and my husband was most indignant when asked if he was responsible.

The bread continued to appear intermittently for some weeks until one day, when entering the kitchen, I froze in amazement and watched the culprit at work. There was our cat Pungu on the bench. She nudged open the wooden roll-top of the bread bin, reached inside with her paw and hooked a slice of bread, which she picked up in her mouth. She then jumped off the bench, ran into the lounge and dropped the bread beside a bemused-looking Jade.

Mystery solved.

Gaynor Ngapo
Tokoroa

A furry nursemaid

We have had numerous pets over the years including a budgie, seven cats, countless guinea pigs, one rabbit and a rainbow lorikeet. (I am not including the goldfish, frogs or snails!) Our own little zoo.

Each pet has been unique and delightful in its own way, providing hours of entertainment over the years.

Our bunny captivated us from the moment we saw him while we were passing a pet shop window, carefully washing his ears and grooming himself like a cat. He was a cross between a Norwegian dwarf and an angora. The result should have been a small fluffy bunny but in Smokey's case he was big, not large, and he had short blue-grey fur with a darker face mask.

To keep Smokey company we bought our daughter a white, crested guinea pig, aptly named Snowy. They were good mates. They both took turns to go to school for visits with the children (yes, I'm a primary school teacher). The children were very good with them, but on one occasion while Snowy was on a visit he was hurt. There was no blood or visible damage but he was obviously badly hurt. He lay quietly in his box and refused to eat or drink anything.

The first night he slept in the hot water cupboard where it was warm. The next day being a Saturday I was home and able to nurse him. He had not moved, wouldn't eat, and was given water from an eye dropper. Late afternoon there was still no change and I thought he was going to die overnight. So I put him, box and all, on the kitchen floor where Smokey was hopping about.

Smokey had obviously missed his little friend because he went straight over and hopped into the box with him. He washed Snowy all over, then lay down with his chin on Snowy's back. I continued to give Snowy water and offer him food, but he lay still, cuddled into his friend. That night I put them both into the cat box so they could stay one last night together.

Next morning I found Snowy sleeping draped over Smokey's tummy. He ate some grass and was at last up on his feet. Smokey kept up the nursing care, keeping him clean and warm. Sometimes I could only see Snowy's cheeky little face peering out from under Smokey's tummy. He would sleep under Smokey's tummy because there it was the warmest.

Snowy lived another four years accompanied by his best friend and protector, but never fully recovered. He had toilet troubles and needed our care daily as well as Smokey's continued nursing and comfort. Smokey saved Snowy's life and showed the same gentle nature to all subsequent guinea pigs, even when overrun by 15 of them, 12 of which were Snowy's offspring.

Jenny Harris
Balclutha

A seeing-eye cat

We've had Bodie since he was a beautiful cocker spaniel puppy at ten weeks old.

We moved into a new house that was part of the package of my husband's employment. As we moved in, much to our surprise so did a lovely cameo-coloured kitten about the same age as Bodie. It took several weeks to figure out that Tozer actually belonged to the neighbour, but the friendship was instant between the two. They played for hours on end, and the entertainment was priceless. 'Chasey' over the beds, up and down the stairs, and when they had had enough fun they would curl up together in Bodie's basket for a sleep. Often they would even share the same feeding bowl.

These two were inseparable. After 18 months another transfer of housing was about to happen and I hated to separate the two, knowing that each one would miss the other. However, a couple of weeks after our move the neighbours phoned to ask if we wanted Tozer as they were going overseas. Of course we didn't hesitate and drove back straight away to pick him up.

These two have been best mates through the years, and are now both aged 13 years. Bodie is both partially deaf and totally blind, and a diabetic to boot. Morning and evening I only need to say 'Walkies time' and Tozer cat is out the gate before Bodie and I. We have

Smarter than Jill

Tozer the cat

become well known in The Parade where we live and I am known as the 'cat lady'.

The amazing thing is that Tozer always walks on the inside of the footpath as Bodie tends to wander to the left, where he can bump into the fences etc; Tozer is ready to keep Bodie on track so gives him a playful smack on the nose to say *Move over*.

I know Tozer is aware of Bodie's blindness, as are the many other dogs we pass on our walks. Tozer is playing his part as 'seeing-eye cat', and when he sees Bodie approaching, he lets out a piercing meow that says *I am right here, please don't stand on me*. This often happens sadly, as Bodie has neither seen nor heard him. Tozer just seems to take it all in his stride and understands the situation.

Both pets go boating with us, and Tozer is an excellent deckhand, always waiting for a feed of fresh fish, and ready to smooch on our leg to say *put a line over, it is getting near dinner time*. I know Bodie's time with us is running out, and I can't imagine life without him. But, for all the extra care and expense his condition has cost, we have been repaid tenfold, for a more affectionate and loving companion would be impossible to find. For the present I try to make the most of the precious time we have left to share.

June Woods
Auckland

A changed cat

Nestles – 'Miss Independent' – was an ordinary black unwanted kitten with an attitude problem. From day one her manner towards us was haughty and she barely tolerated occasional patting. Most of her time was spent in nearby farm paddocks and many a mouse, bird and rabbit were proudly brought home for inspection.

One day Nestles was involved in a fight, unfortunately not a rare occurrence. This time, however, she was clearly the loser. A hurried trip to the vet did nothing to stop the abscess from opening into a huge gaping pus-filled hole. Poor Nestles stank to high heaven.

With the massive wound seeping she showed no inclination to move so a warm draft-free bed was made for her in the garage. During the time it took her body to heal I was in and out all day offering warmed milk, tasty morsels of food and what I hoped were suitable words of comfort for a member of the feline family. Gradually the wound healed and when it did Nestles became a changed cat. Affectionate and loving, she still continued to roam free but obviously also now enjoyed being part of our family.

Some time later I received upsetting news of the terminal illness of a close family member. Nestles sat at my feet as I wept. My husband suggested a hot bath and soon after, lying in the soothing warm water, I heard an awful 'crying'. Nestles was outside the bathroom door making an indescribable noise.

My husband opened the door and she leapt up onto the bath beside me. An experimental paw dabbled in the water, which obviously was not to her liking, whereupon she promptly walked round the side of the bath and curled up close against my neck. When I sat up to let the bath water out she jumped down and stalked out of the room. From that day on every time I took a bath Nestles was in her appointed place – wrapped around my neck.

Cheryll Gadsby
Hawera

Sidee

My friend Karen has always had horses and dogs. She has a special talent for getting the best out of an animal, whether in training or just a good response from a difficult individual.

In 1992 she had a German shepherd cross bitch called Spice, and a young Sibe-bord (Siberian husky border collie cross) called Cruz. She also had a horse called Sidee, so named because he always turned his head to one side.

As she often did, she was out riding Sidee and the dogs were along for company. It was a lovely summer's day and Karen decided they could all do with a cool swim across the river, something that they had done many enjoyable times before.

All went as normal, but suddenly right in the middle of the river, at its deepest, Sidee began to convulse. The poor horse was totally uncontrollable as it heaved and thrashed, and there was not a thing Karen could do to guide it into the shallow water. Within seconds the horse, still flailing, sank.

The water was murky, with foam and mud stirred up from the riverbed with the horse's thrashing. To make matters worse, the current tumbled Sidee over and over. Karen was trapped, vision was nil and the horse's lethal legs and hooves were wildly kicking.

Amazingly Karen didn't panic but became increasingly frightened when she couldn't find a clear way out of the saddle. She couldn't tell which way the surface was and she could see the flailing hooves in the thick murk.

Suddenly a flash of white caught her eye, yes there it was again. Young Cruz was swimming around the horse desperately trying to find his 'Boss'. In desperation Karen made a lunge for the white flag of Cruz's tail end and luckily made contact. With strength born of the will to survive she grabbed with her other hand a bunch of hair on Cruz's back. Good dog, he swam like a Newfoundland straight to the surface and, praise be, no one was kicked by Sidee on the way.

What seemed like an eternity later, Karen reached the shallows and she and both dogs lay exhausted regaining their strength. Spice had also been swimming round and round trying to locate Karen.

As they had ended up on the wrong side of the river Karen realised they would have to swim back across again, even though she felt totally spent. Hoping her loyal dogs had strength enough for all, she caught hold of their collars in each hand and urged them back into the water. What brave, strong friends they proved to be. Of her other companion Sidee there was no sign. A few hours later Karen and the stock control officer, whom she had alerted, found her horse some distance downriver.

The autopsy revealed Sidee had suffered a sudden major brain haemorrhage.

Sadly she laid a good horse to rest, but has memories of two incredible dogs that saved her life.

Joyce Duggan
Tauranga

Fluff the midwife

The year was 1955. Our dear old Fluff cat had two female kittens. Eight months later, one was due to produce, as they do! I was outside, and heard a terrible noise of a cat crying, coming from under a hedge round our home.

I could not believe my eyes at what I was seeing when I went to investigate. Here was dear Fluff, licking the kittens into the world at one end, 'sister' at the other, lying down, with 'mum' stretched out with her head on her stomach, using her for a pillow, and screaming with pain. Five kittens later, all was well. Relieved looks from them all, had to be seen! Who said animals are dumb?!

Gloria Herrick
Tuatapere, Southland

Boy's delight

While mustering sheep I found a very sick sheep with facial eczema, which I immediately put down and buried in a small chasm.

A short time later I put my head and shoulders down a similar chasm to fix a wire to the bottom of a post in a washout. Three of my dogs were asleep close by. Boy was watching me closely, till I partly disappeared down this hole. A few seconds passed, then I felt two heavy taps on my back. I thought, that's Boy, he often tapped my thigh before being fed.

I froze, no movement, no sound came from me, suddenly frantic scratching on my back. I slowly raised my head to see the most unbelievable expression on Boy's face. I was alive, not dead like the sheep he had seen a short time ago. Had I been dead no one would have got near my body.

Boy, a smart and faithful worker for ten years.

Lyndon Evans
Papakura

Gina

Gina was our new kitten. She was beautiful – grey with white front, chin and paws. We wanted a kitten so we chose one, as simple as that! There was no need to ask anyone. We could please ourselves. What freedom!

We had just set up house in our flat – Ronnie, Sue, Jean and I – at Number 2 Willowbank. There were no parents, no landladies, no hostel supervisors telling what we could or could not do. It was a dear little house opposite the Leith Stream, with three bedrooms, a tiny sitting room, a lean-to kitchen stuck on the back and a loo across the yard in a corner. Jean and I had the single rooms as our exams were coming up. We would swot with Ronnie and Sue in August before their finals. We were having an hilariously happy time and Gina's arrival was the final touch.

Gina grew up fast into a cuddly, purry, person-cat. There was always a lap or a warm bed available and she thrived on it. Then suddenly she was in season. Sue knew about these things. I would never have noticed – she seemed to be still a baby herself. We waited in excitement. Then, sure enough she was pregnant.

Unluckily we were all out at lectures the day she gave birth to four perfect kittens: two black, one tabby and one grey and white – a small replica of herself? How would she know how to care for them, being scarcely more that a kitten herself? But she did. She was a wonderful, protective, nurturing mother and we watched in delight.

Then one Saturday Sue went out tramping for the morning on the Taerai. She found a tiny rabbit, only a few days old, lying defenceless in a field. She couldn't leave him there so she bought him home in her hat.

We looked at him with a mixture on wonder and horror. Wonder because he was so like the kittens – only slightly bigger and his ears were different – but, like them, his eyes were still closed. Horror because he was surely in even more danger in our house than in the open field. Gina was a brilliant hunter at any time, and now with her own kittens to protect she would surely kill on sight. We feared for the motherless bunny.

We warmed some milk and did our best to feed him. But it was impossible. We tried and eyedropper but he couldn't swallow. We soaked a handkerchief in the milk but he didn't know what to do with it. We even borrowed a doll's feeding bottle from a little girl we knew, but that was useless too.

The next problem was where to put him till we decided what best to do. After much debate we selected the small high mantelpiece in the kitchen as the safest place. Gina and kittens were in a warm box in the corner of the lounge. There was no was she would find him there and she wouldn't be able to get onto that narrow ledge anyway. So we put him in a soft warm bed in a shoebox.

We then went about our various tasks of a late Saturday afternoon – getting in the washing, cleaning the bathroom, fixing a bike puncture, etc. then one of us went to check the bunny. There was a scream of horror. 'Gina's Killed him'. We all converged on the kitchen. The shoe-box, still high on the mantelpiece, was empty. We couldn't believe it. How absolutely horrible! Our beautiful cat was a monster – a murderer. We looked at each other in despair. What a terrible sequence of events!

We stormed into the sitting room to rage her. But as we looked into the box our mouths dropped open in astonishment. We could not believe our eyes! There lay Gina feeding no four small babies – but five! The extra was just slightly bigger with different ears. We knelt beside them in total awe. We apologised over and over to our wonderful cat and she purred in great contentment and pride. We could hardly comprehend that powerful mothering instinct we saw before us. We couldn't stop gazing at them. We were spellbound.

But the magic didn't last. Gina tried her best but his suckling hurt her nipples and she couldn't manage. We had no choice but to kill him as painlessly as possible and then we sadly buried him in the back garden.

Marion McInnes
Wellington

Khedive, our gentle giant friend

In the first year of our marriage, my husband surprised me one Christmas with the gift of a puppy Afghan hound. The small dog had been flown in from Holland, as in those days it was impossible to get one in New Zealand. We picked him up at the airport, where we also picked up our business guest, the ambassador of the former Czechoslovakia.

Smarter than Jill

The first thing our new puppy did was lift his leg against our esteemed guest's leg!

As Khedive, our hound, grew into a massive and extremely handsome dog, we were having grave personal financial problems and often wondered how to pay for the next meal. That is, until our wonderful dog started to become the main breadwinner, literally! As the local baker popped fresh loaves in his client's letterboxes early in the morning, our pooch followed him, collected the loaves and carefully deposited them in our kitchen. Thirty or forty *NZ Herald*s followed and countless bottles of milk. In the afternoon, of course, he delivered us multiple copies of the *Auckland Star*. The food was never slobbered on, eaten or broken. It arrived in pristine, undamaged condition.

Soon Khedive's ventures produced a wider diet: whole beef or lamb roasts, raw packaged or cooked chickens, large packages of cheese and slabs of chocolate and once even seven live chicks! Becoming bored, he diversified and decided that we obviously also needed clothes. We had the choice of at least 20 pairs of Wellington boots, shoes, overshoes, expensive custom-made straw bowler hats, umbrellas for many rainy days and, to top it off, a couple of live turtles to keep us amused!

Having now a small son and daughter, he was the best nanny possible. Wherever the babies crawled, he followed, picking them up by the back of their domed suits and carting them inside if he thought they ventured too far. When they were due for a nap, he would lie on his side and we would find our children curled up inside his legs, in spoon-like fashion, while our cat completed the picture by curling inside theirs! The whole party snored and whistled happily for a couple of hours on the carpet until one would wake up and mayhem would break loose.

Smarter than Jill

Khedive died of cancer after a few years, but we'll never forget his intelligence, his finely-tuned ability to 'tap' into our moods and play the clown to lift us out of a depression and, most of all, the many wonderful years of friendship he gave us.

Margaretha Western-Brounts
Auckland

7

Smart animals learn fast

The cat who did tricks

I was 14 years old, standing with my father in front of a row of cages at the local SPCA. I was there for a very important reason. I had come to choose a kitten, a chocolate box kitten. And there it was before me, all eyes and fluff and mewing mouth. Perfection!

Gradually, I became aware of a slender paw outstretched from the adjoining cage. I turned and looked into the green eyes of a young cat, well past the cute kitten stage. It was dark-grey and white, with a lop-sided marking running down its nose – definitely not chocolate box. It stared intently at me and again offered its paw. And that was how Bunny came into my life, so named because his fur was thick and soft like a rabbit's.

Bunny was a very loving cat with a great desire to please and we quickly bonded. He soon learnt the school bus routine and every afternoon would take up his position on the front gatepost ten minutes or so before I was dropped off. I taught him to leave his food until I had stroked his head and given the command. I could even leave the room for a few minutes and return to find him waiting patiently for permission to eat.

This unusual cat behaviour led me to go further. The hula hoop craze was in full swing and most of us had bought a strip of cane and made our own. I decided to teach Bunny to jump through the hoop for each piece of meat. He had to walk round the back of me and pass through the hoop, resting upright on the floor, to reach the reward. Over time, I raised the height until he was jumping in fine style.

Now for the finishing touch. Bunny had to learn to jump over the top! I covered the entire opening with paper and again stood it on the ground. If he wanted the meat, he had to jump over. Going round was a no-no. Once he knew and obeyed my instruction 'over the top', I removed the paper and Bunny would then jump through or over on command at whatever height I held it. Mission accomplished! Bunny was a star turn with our visitors.

All these years later, I look at the old black and white photos I have of him performing and realise once again what a unique cat he was.

Carol Ercolano
Nelson

Mighty mouse

I woke one night to say to my wife, 'Did you hear that?'

The sound was similar to that made by our pet white mouse Woody when running on the treadmill in his cage. He had died, and as my daughter had gone off to university around the same time, the cage was stored in her empty bedroom.

My wife told me that I was dreaming and to go to sleep. A little later that night I heard it again. I ran downstairs, convinced I wasn't dreaming. Yet when I turned on the light in the downstairs bedroom – nothing. I checked the cage and still nothing.

We talked about it the next day and my wife was telling me I was dreaming. I thought perhaps she was right.

The next night I heard it again, and after my swift move downstairs with the torch, still nothing. This wasn't going to beat me. So I slept in

Smarter than Jill

Bunny the cat and Carol

the spare bedroom, where the cage was, because I was sure it came from the cage. I had my trusty torch at the ready.

About an hour later, yet again I heard the sound. It was definitely the treadmill. Without a sound I pointed the torch at the cage and turned it on. There to my amazement I saw a little brown field mouse running on the treadmill. When he saw the light he promptly vacated the exercise equipment, squeezed himself through the bars of the cage and hid in the wardrobe.

Now, our Woody took a week to learn the knack of the treadmill, and never tried to squeeze out of the bars. We thought that this little mighty mouse deserved to live and for a week or so after that we would hear the treadmill going on and off most nights.

We never really knew what happened to him after that. Perhaps the novelty of the treadmill wore off and he went on some other adventure.

Andrew and Susan Gawlik
Rotorua

Let there be light

Sheba was a little tortoiseshell cat, dark ash grey and jaffa cream, with a cute little raccoon-mask face . . . as pretty as a picture. But Sheba also had a brain. She did one of the most intelligent things I have ever seen a cat do . . .

One evening I was carrying her and I happened to turn on the laundry light. Sheba watched intently as I touched the switch, and lo, instantly there was light.

She sat very still in my arms, just studying the switch . . .

Some time later I realised that the laundry light was on. Puzzled, I was sure I had turned it off before, but obviously I had not. I switched it off and went back to watch TV.

A while later, it was on again.

I *knew* I had turned it off. I turned out the light and hid behind the door, to see if I could solve the mystery.

Presently I saw Sheba jump up onto the washing machine. She stood up on her hind legs and her forepaws turned on the light. I was fascinated by her intelligence and came out of hiding to give her a cuddle. I had to turn off the light several more times until the novelty wore off for Sheba.

It never ceases to amaze me just how incredibly intelligent animals are. Sheba's logical working out of the situation really impressed me.

Her clever little raccoon-face looked at me as if to say, *I can do that too, you know.*

I felt that it was symbolic . . . how much animals light up people's lives. Their love and trust is our greatest treasure . . .

Let there be light!

Jenny Gregory
Opotiki

A cold cat

A cat Mum used to have would sit in front of the fan heater on a cold morning, look at the plug on the floor, then the socket on the wall and then at Mum. He would keep doing this until she plugged it in.

Owen Goodrick
Tauranga

Jump on the bed, dear

Mhadaidh was very very special. A border collie rough collie cross, she had everything: a lovely temperament and delightful personality, attractive looks with beautiful soft brown eyes. I always felt that the description of Luath, the collie in Robert Burns' poem *The Twa Dogs*, might have been written especially for Mhadaidh. And her intelligence was incredible.

I believe that for a dog to have a vocabulary of 50 or so words is considered good. Mhadaidh's vocabulary was 90 words.

She was a girl of many parts. She could climb a tree, work stock, take messages to people, ride with my son on his motorbike and help me hang out the washing by passing me the pegs or picking up a fallen garment. If I was horse riding and I dropped my stick, or my shady hat blew away, Mhadaidh would return them to me.

One of my favourite memories was one day when I was having a bath, and I discovered that I had left my towel in my bedroom. Mhadaidh was lying on the carpet in the sitting room.

'Beas!' I called. Beas, short for Beasley, was one of several nicknames to which she responded. 'Run up and jump on the bed, dear.'

This is a long command for a dog, but Beas was equal to it, as was Liesl, a Pomeranian I used to own. Sitting there in the water, I heard Mhadaidh's paws going *shuff, shuff* up the passage. On to the bed she leaped.

'Pick it up!' was my next request.

Quite often I didn't even need to name the object. 'Pick it up!' was enough to set my darling looking about her: *What does she want me to fetch now?*

'Pick it up!' I encouraged. 'That's a good girl. You bring 'em!' And sure enough 'bring 'em' she did.

Beasley appeared in the open bathroom doorway complete with towel, her plumy tail a-wag and her clever eyes smiling. My heart

Smarter than Jill

Mhadaidh the dog

swelled with love for her. What praise I lavished on my brainy black and white girl!

If I was, say, cutting thistles, and had left my jersey on the fence, I could always send Mhadaidh to retrieve it for me.

'Fetch jersey!' and off she would streak, the fence maybe 100 metres distant. It impressed me very much that instead of dragging the garment off the wire by the hem, she always used to lift it off – something she worked out for herself.

Unfortunately Mhadaidh is no longer with me. Smart and gentle, brave and beautiful, she was put to sleep at the ripe old age of nearly 15, suffering from arthritis. I still miss her dreadfully.

Chrissy Wade
Paengaroa

Watching alpacas

Most people with pets like to have a rapport with them. They talk about them as their children, often crediting the cat, the dog or the goldfish with a fair slice of intelligence. What many a pet lover would like most is to have them talking back, or at least to know what they think.

Any animal has the ability to produce sound and express itself through body language, which can be not only in the way they stand but also in their actions. The degree of intelligence in animals can be found in how much they communicate or in their ability to solve a problem or to play games.

Do alpacas do this? How intelligent are they really? In my opinion, animals that can solve a problem or develop a game for fun and not for survival are quite intelligent.

Here are some alpaca anecdotes you might enjoy.

'Skiing' on a dirt slope

We had hillside smoothed with a digger, leaving it a very nice ski slope – except it was dirt, not snow. We let the alpacas in this area after some time and they were quite excited about the bare hillside, particularly the dirt, as they love to roll in it.

One of them started to have his dust bath on the top of the slope. While rolling on his back, he skidded slowly down. At the bottom of the hill he looked up, quite puzzled about what had happened, and decided this was fun. Up he trotted again, to repeat the same trick not once but three or four times.

The others watched in amazement and in no time two more discovered this was a fantastic game.

A-maze-ing sense of direction
One of our quarantine areas is like a maze, with many gates, small paddocks, a race going all around it, everything fenced with wire and mesh, and easy to see through. We have it grazed regularly to keep the grass down.

With all areas connected – some with gates open and some leading into a dead corner – one would think it difficult for a three-week-old cria (baby) to find its way out on its own.

Mum had already walked out and the cria could see her through three fences, but no straight way to get to her. It took only three minutes to work it out, by following the fence lines and the open gates – not trying to get to mum in a straight line.

Real water birds
Last December, when the weather finally turned warm and sunny, we moved the females to a paddock with a stream running through it. The new ones didn't know this, but the others did.

One of the new suri females followed them to the stream, where most of them sat down in the water to cool off. Yes, alpacas love water – but the suri types even more so.

Smarter than Jill

Alpacas watching

Sasha waded into the stream until she had her chin just above the water, then rolled over and took a dive. The next moment she walked out of the stream, climbed the bank and jumped from 1.5 metres high into the same spot she'd just vacated, repeating this a couple of times.

She was having a ball, especially when she shook herself out like a dog next to where I was watching her.

Adventure lovers
Observing alpacas is interesting when they are in areas where adventures can be had.

They become bored in small paddocks, as they naturally are browsers and move around a lot, just like goats. One moment they are here, the next they are on the other side of the stream. In small paddocks, a big pile of rocks or compacted dirt will create a playground.

Communication
Ears are an important part of alpaca communication, as is the tail. I have found they recognise colours better than shapes. They also identify each other at a distance and by scent, and they have excellent eyesight and night vision.

Crias can pick out their mothers at a great distance – most likely by colour, body language and individual sounds. In mono-coloured herds, crias sometimes have a problem finding mum, but they always succeed.

Alpacas talk a lot and all have their own voice. The sounds they make can be 'humming' (*mmm mmmmm mmmm*) or screeching when upset, an 'orgle' by males when mating, a whinny sound for alarm, a keening sound when sad or lonely and clucking sounds when calling to the crias.

There is so much more to know about these amazing animals – if only for their behaviour and, in my humble opinion, their intelligence!

Jeanette Klomp
Aurora Alpacas
Kawakawa, Bay of Islands

As silly as sheep?

I once knew a flock of sheep that knew more about aeroplanes than many humans.

When I was a small child Dad had a small flock of stud Cheviot sheep, elegant animals with clean faces framed by Elizabethan ruffs of fleece and the athletic prowess of miniature deer.

Much of the year they lived on the airstrip, directly across the creek from the house, where they were handy to keep an eye on.

This was back when aerial topdressing, as an industry, was just beginning to lose its 'Cowboys with Wings' image, and aircraft were just beginning to be specially designed and built for the task, rather than being any-old-motor with wings that someone thinking to start up such an operation might be able to scratch up. As a result, there were quite a number of different makes and models of planes operating in our rural community.

Dad was fascinated by these flyboys and their machines. Having one of the first airstrips in the district many of them worked off his strip doing work for other local farmers and he got to know many of the pilots very well.

One of these pilots in particular was a good mate of his. On many days conditions packed in and work was not possible. This pilot would land on the strip and come over the house for a yarn with Dad.

A young chap down the road used to drive the loader for this pilot. I think it was Dad's idea that, rather than the young chap have a long drive to wherever they were going to work, he should just drive by our strip to clear it, and be picked up from there by the pilot.

And where do the sheep come into this?

Well, as I already said, the Cheviot ewes used to live on the strip much of the time. In those days thistles were a real problem, but Dad kept the airstrip mowed clear of them so it could be used at any time. The clear area was the favourite haunt of the sheep.

Usually the young loader-driver would arrive before the plane and drive up and down a few times to chase the sheep off the runway, but he was also helping milk cows sometimes the pilot arrived first. This often being just after daylight, the pilot would fly a couple of low passes up the strip to clear it so he could land, before Dad could arrive over the gully to clear it for him.

It didn't take very long for the sheep to cotton on to the fact that the sound of the plane's motor meant a rude awakening was in the offing. Before long they would move off the strip as soon as they heard the sound of that plane.

Now, as I said, at that time there were quite a number of different makes of aircraft being used as aerial topdressing planes and by now there was more than one airstrip in the district. On some days at certain times of the season it was not uncommon for there to three or four different aircraft of different makes working the district. The Cheviots would continue to graze quite unconcerned, but if a particular plane were in the area, they would file off the runway in very short order.

What really proved to Dad how well the sheep could tell the different planes apart was the day he knew his mate was working elsewhere, out of the district. There was another working locally that day, ignored by the sheep.

Suddenly, just on lunchtime, they all suddenly rushed off the runway, and moments later a plane appeared low from behind the trees, touched down and stopped fast. Dad's pilot mate had struck trouble, headed for home and deciding that he wasn't going to make it he headed for the safest strip on his line of flight, Dad's.

We'd heard the plane coming and assumed it was the other one working in the area that day, but the sheep knew different. From the way they cleared the strip in a hurry I wouldn't mind betting they knew he was in trouble and only had the one shot of getting on to the deck.

That pilot's gone to the great airfield up yonder now, and Dad's retired to town, but I've never forgotten the sheep that knew their aircraft.

Gayle Cresswell
Woodville

A true sheepdog

Some years ago I decided that pet lambs were no longer an option for me and in the future they would be the total responsibility of my grandchildren. However, providence has a way of changing these plans.

It was school holidays when I was presented with a small white woolly waif and, with the grandchildren all away on holiday, it fell to me to feed it. With some resentment I began this task.

The bundle of wool, called Lolliper, had a personality all its own and she had soon won me over. Perhaps because she was an 'only'? Or just perhaps because she was very self-possessed, this lamb became an attachment.

At the time I also had two dogs, one of which, a beautiful golden Great Dane, had a very large closed-in room-like kennel, outside which was a concrete step. A very unusual bonding took place between the dog and the lamb, who took to sleeping on the doorstep of the kennel.

When we went for a walk, she always came too and it was a wonderful friendship.

However, at first we did not fully realise the extent of the beliefs of the lamb as she grew older, until one day when my son was bringing a mob of sheep past the gate and she rushed out to round them up in the manner of a dog.

Without knowing, we had a real sheepdog!

Sonia Mackenzie
Napier

He's not so silly

Our lovely ginger cats Cagney and Lacey are getting older. Once they regularly caught small animals and birds and brought them to us. Now they catch less and sometimes the poor things are still alive when presented. The cats seem incapable of catching them a second time when they release them.

As a result we have passed many a frustrating hour chasing things out of the house.

I was working on the computer one evening and turned on the printer. It made the usual clanging noise all cheap printers make as they set up and Cagney came running.

He sat in front of the machine and waited. I pretty much ignored him and after an hour or so he left.

The next night, with the accompanying racket, I turned on the printer. Cagney came running again. As he took up position in front of the printer I took a bit more notice. If nothing else, he is a pretty laid-back cat, used to his every whim being satisfied. Running was out of character! Eventually he went away.

This continued for five nights and I must admit to being intrigued. He just sat there.

On the sixth night I turned on the printer and waited for him to come running. It had become instinct for me too! As he took up his post I laughed and told him, 'The mouse is on the mousepad and it's not real you know.'

What do I know! Next thing the printer whirrs into action and out pops a tiny field mouse straight into Cagney's waiting embrace.

Jenny Barlow
Tauranga

Marvellous Martin

Long ago in the late '60s and in a place far away (California), my young bride and I became the parents of a kitten that we named Martin Luther Cat. Since we were about to go on our honeymoon, we had to train him to come to my whistling.

We intended to travel from California to Florida in a camper with Martin as company. Each time we made a rest stop or camped for the night, we trusted that Martin would return when I whistled. Sure enough, over our circuitous route from California through Illinois down to Florida and then back, Martin stayed with us. As I have since found out, cats think that people are their family, and if you feed them, they bond with you as the papa cat and mama cat.

Smarter than Jill

Alone, camping by lakes and streams, we spent a lot of time petting our cat and talking to him. Martin was good company and very loyal so when we returned to California and found a new home, he settled right in. He always watched everything we did, and like all observant cats, he followed our routines. He knew that we would hurry to the phone when it rang or we would go and open the door when someone knocked. He watched us, and of course, during his studies, he discovered everything about getting fed and where we kept his food.

Every weekday, my wife and I would go off to teach, leaving Martin at home. Having this empty apartment to himself must have been a big challenge for Martin. He must have felt responsible to carry on for us since he took on answering the phone and opening the front door. Coming home from school and finding the door open or the phone off the hook I just dismissed as carelessness until the day I phoned home, and after a few rings the phone was answered and a meow was heard. I had to see this for myself so I went home and waited for my wife to call. She called, and let the phone ring. After it went for quite a while, Martin came charging around a corner, jumped up on the hall table, stood on his rear paws, and using his front paws pushed the receiver off the hook. As if that feat was not enough, he put his nose to the mouthpiece and meowed.

So there it was, the handset lying on the hall table and Martin meowing into it.

Seeing a cat on the phone was incredible, but he topped it one day when I didn't get to the front door in time and found him swinging with both paws clenched around the knob. The knob was the old style with a relief engraved into it for traction. Martin was able to hang on as he swung from side to side until the knob turned and the door opened.

Marvellous Martin was a stunner.

He travelled with us for the rest of his life, finally settling on our farm in Maui, Hawaii. He stopped answering phones and opening doors, but hearing the upstairs toilet flush, my wife and I just shook our heads and smiled, 'Oh, Marvellous Martin, you're at it again.'

Mike Ward
Mangonui

Thinking sheep

I've heard it said by some that sheep are stupid. Stupid? How come? Well, they say, they walk across paddocks in single file. Excuse me?! Of course they do. How else ought they walk? And wouldn't you, on a mountain? Because sheep, you see, have their origins in mountains. And on a mountain you would look pretty silly creeping about its sides in a cluster. Do human beings climb up mountains in clusters? Did Sir Ed reach the top of Mount Everest in a cluster? No. He went up . . . and down . . . in single file. Had he done it any other way he probably would have fallen off, a fact worked out by sheep in the hidden mists of time.

In any case who are we to laugh at sheep for their single-fileness. We are rather apt to create little tracks everywhere too. Look at our roads. What are they but tracks upon which we sally forth in single file? And when we take a stroll through the nearest bush we tend to stick to the beaten path and are usually to be found walking in . . . yes, single file, like a flock of sheep.

When you live on a sheep farm and deal with sheep every day you soon learn that they are individual creatures. Some are thinkers, some are not . . . just like people.

Take Tully, for example. Recently Tully, a rather rotund Romney mother of many, fixed her gleaming eyes upon an especially tantalising leaf or two of oak tree above her head. She stood on her hind legs but the branch remained just out of mouth's way. Tully thought. She looked this way. She looked that way. She looked up. She looked down. She considered. Then she paced backwards. One, two, three, four, five, six. Stopped. Looked up at the branch, then down at the ground, quite obviously judging distance. Took a deep breath, then ran as fast as her fat little legs would take her, launched herself in the air, grabbed the branch with her teeth, down to the ground with it and before it could fly up again she stood on it firmly and began plucking those delicious morsels.

Now if that's not using one's intelligence . . .!

And let me introduce you to Daisy, a Drysdale sheep. Daisy used her considerable intellect to observe human life, especially the way it lay in comfort on a couch. She caught a mere glimpse of this phenomenon before being rudely swept out of sight by a broom. Still, one glimpse was enough for this Mensa IQ. The next day, there she lay sprawled out on the sofa chewing the cud and being cuddled by two contented farm cats. And how did she get herself into the house? Well, from observation Daisy knew how to unlatch the garden gate and the house door.

When she became a mother Daisy usually enjoyed that role but had reservations the year the Hulks were born. Male twins, the Hulks were troublemakers from the start and very demanding on their mother. When they grew almost as big as she but continued in their insatiable desire for milk . . . lifting their mother completely off the ground as they butted at her udder . . . Daisy lost patience. She marched them down the farm road, waited until they were engrossed in nibbling tasty grass seed heads, then ran all the way back up the road to the house paddock and hid behind a shed, scoring for herself at least an hour of peace before the Hulks 'sprung' their dozing mum.

Smarter than Jill

No doubt about it. Sheep are intelligent creatures. Scientists have even proved that many sheep have more brainpower than many dogs.

Of course scientists have also proved that pigs are even more intelligent than either sheep or dogs . . . But that's another story.

Mary Purchas
Tauranga

8

Smart animals go for help

A cat having a rest

That swampy paddock

One Sunday morning a few years back, my Dad and I went onto the farm to move some animals. We eventually got to the last job: moving some cows out of a swampy paddock.

We sent the dogs round and slowly the cows all headed towards the gate, all except one. A black cow stood on the other side of the swamp. She stood staring at us, constantly mooing and not moving an inch. The dogs ran at her, barking and jumping, yet still she didn't flinch. Finally Dad got impatient, and we drove around the swamp towards the cow.

Smarter than Jill

We reached her, wondering why she hadn't moved. She mooed again and to our amazement, she leaned her head towards something in the swamp. We leaned towards the swamp and beneath us, neck-high in mud, was a sheep. We began digging and pulling at it and only after some time did it come free of the mud.

At this stage the cow stopped mooing and began trotting around the side of the swamp and out the gate. The sheep stood slowly and stumbled away from where fate had meant it to die that day!

Every time I enter that same paddock, I flashback to that day and think of the courage, bravery and intelligence that the cow showed, all to help a fellow farm mate.

Lydia Cave
Wanganui

Come back here

Mum had spring and autumn calvers, and when they were due to give birth, they would be shifted into the paddock in front of the house, where Mum could keep a close eye on them.

One day, one of the Hereford cows that had a calf that was three days old positioned herself by the house fence and proceeded to bellow for quite some time. Realising something was wrong, Mum went to check on her. She was obviously all right, but went over to inspect her calf that was curled up asleep. The cow followed Mum over, stood by her calf and persisted in bellowing, looking at Mum, then at her calf. To Mum, the calf seemed fine, just sleeping, so she returned to the house, satisfied all was in order.

However, the cow followed Mum back, and promptly took up her station by the fence and continued to bellow.

After a few more minutes of this, Mum decided something must be amiss so returned to take a closer look at the calf. When she lifted it to its feet, she discovered it was scouring badly and listless.

Mum had to apologise to the cow and walked through the paddock to the yards with the cow in hot pursuit. She waited at the gate for Mum to return with the medicine and stood over her as she administered it to the calf.

Once this had been done, the cow was satisfied and lay down beside the calf to keep her bedside vigil. Mum didn't hear from her again.

Fleur and Tina Cushman
South Auckland

Reubin the horse

It was in the first year of our ten-year stint in Botswana that we were offered land on an old wild game farm to establish a stable yard. The farm had been closed to the public for some years but the animals still remained. We had no qualms about the kudu, impala, warthogs, vultures, etc that roamed the lands, not even the lions (they were safe behind their own high fences) but we did worry about the herd of wild horses causing mayhem with our domestic horses. As it turned out they were wilder than the wild game and quickly bolted off at the sight of man and rider.

The animal snaring on the lands was a big problem and the farm owner welcomed our presence on his deserted lands as he assumed that having the farm occupied would dissuade the trappers from roaming too freely. His worries having been sorted out, we turned to ours concerning the wild horses.

The blot on our idyllic landscape became the annual round-up of the wild herd for their 'African Horsesickness' injections. They were a vicious lot and we all agreed we'd rather spend a night in the lion pens than in a yard with the wild herd. It was all hands on deck for the round-ups. Once we got them into the stable yard the object was to get them through the 'cattle crush' as quickly as possible, injecting them wherever we could reach. The local vet wisely stayed well away from this circus!

I liked to arrive for my afternoon stable check when the grooms were out collecting our horses for their afternoon groom. As I drove in one balmy afternoon I immediately saw an unknown horse standing in the stable yard – a horse I soon recognised as one of the wild herd. I approached him with my heart in my throat, which quickly turned to a retching in my throat as the smell of rotten flesh emanated from him into the afternoon air. He stood passively and haughtily as I made soothing noises (more for myself than for the horse I think).

The bile rose along with anger when I saw that he was dragging a snare complete with part of a tree stump behind him. How he had found the strength to dislodge the stump we would never know, nor could we imagine the pain he would have been in.

The wire from the snare was embedded bone deep and the flies and maggots were dropping off the putrid flesh. He stood quietly as I cut in with the fence cutters to remove the wire and then as I bathed the wound and pulled out maggots and dirt. Maggots are actually very good for a wound as they assist in cleaning it out but this wound was too terrible for even the maggots to cope with.

This brave wild horse stood quietly in the yard for eight days whilst his wound was tended to and massive doses of antibiotic were injected into his body (again the local vet gladly supplying the medicine needed but staying well away). One afternoon I arrived and he had gone just as quietly as he had arrived. I saw him a few days later with the wild herd but as I approached he took off with the herd with not even a backward glance. He behaved as if he had never had close contact with a human, and was just as vicious as before his snaring experience when they were rounded up for their next 'African Horse-sickness' jab.

It would have been forgivable if I had felt hurt at being treated with such disdain by the big black horse but instead I was overcome with a feeling of immense gratitude that although he had come to humans for help in his time of need he had not done so at the cost of his spiritual freedom. He had certainly gained my respect for his intelligence, trust and spirit.

Wendy Roberts
Lower Hutt

Going for help

My husband was tidying up the sheep yards after docking and the ewes and lambs were dispersing round the paddocks, when he noticed a distressed-looking ewe coming back and baaing to him repeatedly. He went to see what was wrong and she led him, constantly looking over her shoulder to see if he was following, to a deep ditch, where her lamb (and another one) had fallen in. He was able to rescue them both and the reunited family went happily away.

Who says sheep are dumb!

Margaret Moje
Northland

Amazing Oscar

I hadn't eaten dinner, so later that night I put the grill on and made a couple of pieces of toast. It would have been around 10 pm. I let Oscar my little wire-haired terrier out, ate my toast and watched TV for a while. Opened the back door, 'Come on in Osc, bedtime.' Put the lights off and went in the bedroom.

Oscar sleeps, as always, on the bed in the crook of my legs. We must have dozed off more or less straight away.

I was awakened with his snout nudging my arm, and said 'Come on Osc, you've not long been out, go to sleep.' But persistent he was. He stood at the side of the bed and kept giving me a nudge and running to the door. After five nudges I got up, thinking he must be desperate to go out.

I opened the kitchen door and my eyes widened to a brilliant orange glow; it was like getting off a plane at Bangkok airport, the heat hit me. I'd left the grill on, and with the thermostat not working it had been on full heat since I made the toast. I quickly turned the stove off at the mains. It was so hot it had scorched the wall behind the stove.

I'm certain if Oscar hadn't woken me, in another half an hour, the house would have gone up in flames. When I'd seen to it my little dog went back to bed – he didn't want to go out, he knew something was wrong.

I believe my dog was sent to me for a purpose. He's nearly 11 now and not too good at times. He's made me laugh just about every day and I love him dearly.

Denise Hurt
Papakura

Ewe needing help?

Most people seem to think all sheep are completely stupid. No sheep farmer, and in particular any who have had pet lambs about the place, would agree. When in 1989 I purchased a farmlet and moved from the city I too was of the opinion sheep were rather dim. I learned differently when I was given a year-old ewe who'd been a pet but was now surplus to requirements.

Ellie was an odd shape, rather like the dachshund version of a sheep, but she had two good lambs every year until she died last season, and I'm going to miss her. She was lead sheep for the flock, kept them mostly out of trouble, and was very useful all round. But the incident which opened my eyes to the mental possibilities of a sheep occurred a few years back.

It was lambing time. Early morning, and I was hand-milking my house cow in the bail. Ellie appeared by the gate and baa'd urgently. I looked up. She baa'd again. I continued to milk. Just Ellie communicating, I assumed, she did that. The next baa had an edge on it. What was I? Stupid? I was required, now!

I looked up to see an almost desperate urgency on her face, and the final baa sounded strangled. I had to help, that's what I was for! Realising that there really was something wrong, I rose from the milking stool and followed. Ellie led me around the outside of my trellised park area, down the fence line and along under the shelter belt. Then she halted, looked down and positively bellowed.

Here! This was the problem! *Do* something!

From where I stood I could see only a large branch on the ground, one of the few still left there after the shelter belt had been recently trimmed back. I walked to the spot and looked down. Ellie was right, we did have a problem. Lying helplessly under the branch was Ellie's newborn lamb. It had rolled after birth and was trapped under the branch, unable to stand or escape, and Ellie couldn't reach it. I heaved up the branch, scooped the lamb to safety and restored it to Ellie.

So much for the stupidity of sheep. Ellie had realised her lamb was trapped and she was unable to free it unaided. She had heard me talking to Bet as I milked. Ellie had then not only come to fetch me and lead me back to where the lamb lay. But she'd also been able to sequence thought. The human cares for us; if I bring her, the human will help my lamb. She hadn't merely waited by the lamb and called. She'd come some distance and around a couple of corners, to fetch me. I tell people about Ellie and her lamb. Some are surprised, none of those however are sheep farmers.

Lyn McConchie
Norsewood

A cow in need

We have half a dozen cattle at a time on our smallholding. Two years ago we had five steers that would approach the fence and accept a willow frond or a piece of poplar, but one was very shy and nervous and would never come near us.

One day I was looking over the fence when the shy one came from the far side of the paddock and straight up to me. I saw what I thought was a long stick in its mouth. But I realised it was a stiff stalk of dock stuck up its nose. I reached over and pulled out the stalk, and blood and pus poured out. It tossed its head a few times and went quickly to the trough, where it drank thirstily. The stalk must have been there for some time and desperation made it approach me.

I would like to add that it became friendly, but no – it never approached the fence again. It left me, though, with a high regard for the basic intelligence of cattle.

Imelda Widdowson
Hibiscus Coast

9

Smart animals show cunning and have fun

The tiger and Lynne

A playful tiger

The Wellington zoo seemed very alive, magical and different when I was younger. The female tiger got to know me from my twice-weekly visits (from saving my lunch money), and would deliberately splash me with water from her swimming pool as I walked past. I'd reciprocate with the hose and a water fight would break out. I always lost and I'd go home with my school uniform soaking wet. It was worth the strapping I got.

Lynne Rait
Wellington

The useful cat flap

Our late basset hound, Longfellow Mademoiselle Melina (known to her friends as Cujo), was a couch potato but no mental slouch. She showed this one day when she wasn't allowed inside with her favourite toy, a monkey which had a habit of shedding its stuffing.

My wife Raewyn was hosting a meeting of fellow teachers at our home that afternoon, so had everything spotless before she went to work. That meant Cujo, who was standing at the back door and scratching to be let in, was repeatedly told that she could not come inside with the monkey, which she had in her mouth.

Eventually, answering the umpteenth scratch, Raewyn saw that the monkey had disappeared, opened the door and let Cujo in. She fairly flew inside, sprinted to the cat flap (which she could only get her nose through) on the other side of the house, where she had deposited the monkey, snatched it up and charged across the living room, liberally sprinkling stuffing all the way.

>Peter Jackson
>Kaitaia

Avian logistics

My mother was one of seven sisters, so in my earlier years I was well endowed with aunts. Two of these never married and lived together in a house at the far end of a Cheshire country lane. Their garden was small but attractive, and a haven for a wide variety of birds, especially as the aunts fed them regularly.

When I was first told about *the* sparrow's performance I was not sure as to whether it was an early symptom of dementia or that the old dears had taken to the turps. However, within a week I had to eat my words when I saw it for myself.

The aunts used to spend hours threading peanuts on cotton threads so that these strings of nuts could be hung on the shed spouting, thereby presenting a meal to the blue tits who could hang onto the cotton and feed. The hungrier and greedier sparrows could not perform this feat of gymnastics due to their clumsier feet and had to wait below for any bits which may fall, that is all except *the* sparrow who had figured out a way to beat the system.

He perched on the spouting and leaned over. Unable to reach the nearest nut, he took the cotton in his beak and hauled it up. Placing his foot on the bight of cotton he leaned over again and repeated the manoeuvre, heaving up bight after bight of cotton until he had the nuts, then gorged himself on the proceeds. He repeated this performance day after day for several months, while the aunts gleefully spent a fair proportion of their waking hours threading more and more nuts.

Mike Parry
Dunedin

A pig in the bed

I grew up on a sheep station in the '50s and '60s in the southern Hawkes Bay. Dad was the farm manager and we lived at the end of a country road in the foothills of the Ruahines. Mutton was our staple diet, but each year Dad would buy a weaner pig from the sale yards and it would be fed up to become pork. Dad didn't like us making pets of the farm animals and the pigs were no exception.

One year when I was 10 or 11 we had a black, brown and white pig and, possibly because he was different to the usual white pigs, my brothers and I secretly befriended him. He was soon following us about as we did our chores and taking part in our usual country adventures and games. We called him Percy and he was so tame that he did tricks and would obey most of the commands that we used for the dogs. By some mischance Percy did not go to the works at the porker size and grew large and friendly and I thought he was beautiful.

He would roam at will about the house paddocks, sheds, etc but was not allowed through the garden gate into my mother's large and productive garden. The gate worked on a swing system with a weight so that as you walked through it would automatically swing shut and to lock it there was a hook, which was rarely used. Unbeknown to us Percy had learnt the knack of pushing the gate open to go in and somehow of pulling it to exit without help. The possums were often blamed for what turned out to be Percy's eating of the vegetables.

This day our whole family was at the school agriculture day and Mum was on the cake stall, when the grocer arrived with a story. He did home deliveries to all the farms and used to put our groceries on the kitchen table every Thursday. No locked doors in those days. When he carried the groceries through the garden gate at our house he saw the pig in the garden. He left the door open while he put the groceries on the table and Percy went inside after him!

The grocer chased Percy around and around the dining room and lounge. He said Percy never stepped on the rugs or broke anything, although he did leave a couple of 'stress packets' during the chase. Finally the grocer managed to chase Percy outside and shut the door. Then he couldn't find Percy anywhere in the garden so the grocer left and then told Mum all about it in front of everyone at the school – Horrors!!!

We arrived home, cleaned up the stress mess and tried to find Percy, but we couldn't find him anywhere. We called and called and searched all over the place, but apart from some evidence of snacking in the garden he was nowhere to be found. Banging his food bucket didn't help because he was full of fresh vegies. At last Mum called us in for tea and as we stood on the veranda taking our boots off I gave a few last 'Percy' shouts. One of my brothers went '*Shh* listen.' . . . Nothing. 'Call again.' 'Percy' – grunt, 'Percy' – grunt . . . but where was the grunt coming from?

My brother found him first and quietly called us to come and look. There was Percy sprawled out full length on my brother's bed with his head on the pillow, fast asleep. My brother's bedroom door opened off the veranda and Percy must have pushed the door open and gone in for a nap. When I called 'Percy' he would softly grunt without even opening an eye! Cameras weren't used much then so there is no photo but it will never be forgotten by our family or our small farm community that Pauls have pigs in their beds!!!

Lois Waugh
Levin

A bullying crow

While living in Australia we used to go fishing in our dinghy in the rivers. One day we caught a catfish, which we threw in the water. Quick as a flash a sea hawk dived down and grabbed it, and flew off with it under a tree and started to eat it.

A crow up in the tree was throwing down sticks on it, hoping to drive it away, so it could get the fish for itself.

A station lad told us if you lie down under a tree to rest, the crows will drop sticks on you to see if you're dead.

Sylvia Haff
Putaruru

Smarter than Jill

Don't miss the train!

Older folk will recall the days when trains between Wellington and Auckland used to stop at Taumarunui for 'ten minutes for refreshments'.

There was just time to dash into the tearooms, order a cup of tea and a pie or slice of fruit cake and leap back onto the train. I wasn't the only passenger who'd occasionally souvenir a Railways cup and saucer for my flat. They are long gone but lately I've seen these cups highly priced in antique shops.

The former New Zealand broadcaster Frank Harding once told a friend of mine about a parrot which lived in the Taumarunui tearooms many years ago.

Just as people started queuing at the counter, intent on getting their cuppa, the parrot would let out a loud noise – an exact imitation of the sound made by a train taking off from the platform. Naturally everyone ran frantically outside in pursuit of the train . . . which was, of course, still at rest. Left behind in the tearooms, the parrot would cackle heartily, showing it knew exactly what it had done.

Patricia Reesby
Wellington

Mouse trap

Of the ten cats who have shared our lives, Eddie was the most intelligent. His mother was a petite grey tabby and, according to the vet, his father had to be a Burmese. Like a tui, he had a white tuft under his chin, but he was the archetypal black cat.

Early one summer evening my husband and I noticed a rippling motion under one of the mats in our living room. At that moment,

Eddie came though the cat door and we could see one of our neighbours' white mice in his mouth, the poor creature's tail dangling down one side. We watched, fascinated, as in one deft movement Eddie lifted the corner of the mat and opened his mouth, so that the mouse had no option but to join his partner. The mat was dropped back into place and, satisfied that his second catch was secure, he left.

Businesslike, Eddie was heading off back down the drive when we intercepted him. How dare we? He was indignant, but he accompanied us as we returned the mice to their owners. It was then discovered that the cage with the white mice in it had been temporarily placed in the garage, but was overturned. No one knew how.

We often wondered what Eddie intended to do with his captives, but he never had the opportunity to show us.

Heather Hardiman
Auckland

The sparrows' dilemma

We read about cats and dogs with their clever little ways – well, this is about our common little sparrow.

It being springtime, these two sparrows got together and started building their nest. In my neighbour's guttering of course, as sparrows always seem to do.

They were busily flying around collecting bits and pieces and placing it all together. Now, along came a pair of starlings and drove the poor little sparrows away and took over the building of the nest.

I kept looking out my window, feeling so sorry for the wee birds. I needn't have felt sorry at all.

Within about ten minutes they came flying back, with about eight of their friends. You could almost see the determination in their flight and on their little faces. Now, did they give those starlings some hurry-up. There was a lot of chattering going on. Eventually the starlings were beaten and had to leave.

Anyway, to make a sad story happy, the wee sparrows got their home back. Their little friends all flew away again.

So, you see, even birds help each other.

I think this holds a good moral. Don't be bullies, and help your friends.

Stella Astill
Hamilton

Give a dog a bone

Judy and Cassius (Clay), mother and son, were Foxie-cross dogs, both being very fond of their daily bones.

When they were on holiday at the beach they had to be tied up when outside. They would take it in turns to be either on the long rope, which enabled them to go up the steps across the concrete terrace to the front door, or on the chain, which only allowed them to reach the top of the steps.

One day Judy, who was on the chain, received her bone and settled down on the grass for a quiet chew. Cassius, however, decided that mum's bone looked better than his, and after a few chews on his own took hers and retreated as far as he could go, out of reach of Judy up by the front door.

Judy, needless to say, was not best pleased and set off after him, only to be brought up short at the top of the steps. At this point she picked up his rope in her teeth and going down the steps took his rope around the veranda post and onto the lawn. Here, using the post as leverage, she proceeded to pull.

Poor Cassius, try as he might, could not obtain any grip with his claws on the concrete and, still gripping his mother's bone in his teeth, was pulled ignominiously off the terrace and down the steps. Whereupon his mother reclaimed her bone from him and resumed her chewing.

Barbara Connell
Auckland

Bouncing dog

One morning when I went into our bedroom to make the bed I found Paddy the dog bouncing all over it. He thought his new trampoline was wonderful!

Beth Muir
Dargaville

An eight-footed friend

Is it possible for a spider to relate in a friendly way to a human? Does a spider have the ability to be playful?

I would have said, 'Oh, come on!' until one day when I was working at the bench in my kitchen and felt as if I were being watched. I noticed a spider – one of the little jumping kind – sitting on the windowpane in front of me. Playfully, I flicked a few drops of water onto the glass. The spider hurried after the nearest drop and caught it in his front legs as it slid down. Unfortunately, the drop was heavier than the spider and he was carried down with it to the window sill. He seemed to like this game and returned for two more 'rides' until I decided I had more important things to do than play with a spider!

The next day he was there again. This time he jumped from the windowpane and landed on the rim of the bowl in which I was stirring a cake mix. This was no accidental leap as it was repeated three times over the next few days. He kept me company at food preparation time every day for a week, and then his visits stopped. Perhaps he had been taken by a predator, or had just reached the end of his spider lifespan.

A few weeks later I was painting window frames in the spare bedroom when I noticed a spider sitting on the glass in front of me. It looked just the same as my kitchen buddy, but I knew it was unlikely to be. And all jumping spiders look pretty much alike, except perhaps to another of the same species.

'You'd better not stay there, old chap,' I said to him, 'or you're going to get stuck in the wet paint.' Fortunately there was no one around to hear me talking to a spider, and possibly cart me off somewhere for assessment. I flicked the little fellow onto the floor, out of harm's way. Seconds later he was climbing up the leg of the step stool on which I was standing! Another flick, and I then moved the steps along and started painting the next section of window frame.

Yes, there he was again, climbing up the steps towards me. Maybe word had been passed around on the 'web' that I was good for a bit of entertainment.

'This is daft,' I thought, scooped up the spider on a piece of newspaper and shook him outside.

I may have offended him as I never saw him again.

Anne Martin
Kumeu, Auckland

Afterword

We hope you've enjoyed *Smarter than Jill*. It's been an inspirational and entertaining book to create. Here's a bit of a story about how the smart animal books came to be.

Until late 1999 my life was a seemingly endless search for the elusive 'fulfilment'. I had this feeling that I was put on this earth to make a difference, but I had no idea how. This all left me feeling rather frustrated, lonely and unhappy. I'd always had a creative streak and loved animals. In my early years I spent many hours designing things such as horse saddles, covers and cat and dog beds. I even did a stint as a professional pet photographer.

Then I remembered something I was once told: do something for the right reasons and good things will come. So that's what I did. I set about starting Avocado Press and creating *Smarter than Jack*. All the profit was to go to the SPCA.

Good things did come. People were thrilled to be a part of the book, and many were first-time writers. Readers were entertained and many were delighted to receive the book as a gift. It was short-listed for the Bookseller's Choice Award 2003. The SPCA was over $43,000 better off and I received many calls, letters and emails from people with other ideas they would like to see come to life. What could be better than that?

How could I stop there! It was like I had created a living thing with Avocado Press; it seemed to have a life all of its own. I now had the responsibility of evolving it. It had to continue to benefit society by providing entertainment, warmth and something that people can feel part of. What an awesome responsibility and opportunity, albeit a bit of a scary one!

Avocado Press, as you may have guessed, is a little different. We are about more than just creating books; we're about sharing information, experiences, and developing things in innovative ways. One way we do this is by partnering with other organisations on specific projects to reach like-minded customers; for example, the SPCA. It's a model that everyone benefits from.

We feel it's possible to run a successful business that is both beneficial to customers and gives back to the community. We want people to enjoy and talk about our books; that way, ideas are shared and the better it becomes for everyone.

Jenny Campbell
Avocado Press

Future books you can be involved in

We've got big plans for the future. The next book will have quirky, informative, humorous and obscure questions and answers about animal-related issues. It will be as much for entertainment as for information and should appeal to everyone with an interest in animals. Publication is planned for 2004.

Your questions about animals are now being sought. They could relate to things such as animal etiquette in public, food, behavioural issues, training, breeding, health remedies, pet selection and how to spot a really smart animal! We will then ask the public to offer solutions to the questions that you pose.

To support this book and others we have created a *Smarter than Jack* web site where you can discuss ideas, submit questions and answers, vote on stories and read entertaining and interesting animal news. Check it out at www.smarterthanjack.com.

We're doing more books about smart animals too, including one in Australia.

To submit a story or a question have a look at the next couple of pages, they contain all you need to know. Good luck!

Lastly, we'd love to hear your ideas on what you would like to read and write about in the future and how to make the next books even better.

Submit an animal question

Here's how to go about sending us an animal question:
1. The question should include a bit of an explanation about how the issue came about, like a mini-story. The public will later be asked to submit answers to selected questions.
2. Ideally the questions should be one or two paragraphs long. They may be edited before publication.
3. Photographs and illustrations are welcome if they help demonstrate the question at hand, and if used will appear in black and white.
4. Mark clearly on your submission which book it is for.
5. Submissions can be sent by email or post. Remember to include your name, postal and email address and phone number, and indicate if you do not wish your name to be included with your story.

   Email: submissions@avocadopress.com. A plain text file or email body is preferred, but MS Word formats are fine too.

   Post: Send to Avocado Press, PO Box 22003, Khandallah, Wellington, New Zealand. Handwritten submissions are perfectly acceptable, but if you can type them, so much the better.
6. Posted submissions will not be returned unless a stamped self-addressed envelope is provided.
7. The deadline for submissions is January 31, 2004.
8. The writers of questions selected for publication will be notified prior to publication.

9. Questions are welcome from everybody, and given the charitable nature of our projects there will be no prize money awarded, just recognition for successful submissions.
10. The SPCA and Avocado Press have the right to publish extracts from the stories received without restriction of location or publication.

Have a look at the web site for ideas, sample stories and online entry: www.smarterthanjack.com.

Your details here:

Name: _____

Address: _____

City: _____

Telephone: _____

Email address: _____

Question title: _____

Submit a smart animal story

Here's how to go about sending us a smart animal story:
1. The stories must be true and should be about 200 to 1000 words in length. They may be edited for publication.
2. Photographs and illustrations are welcome if they enhance the story, and if used will appear in black and white.
3. Mark clearly on your submission which book it is for.
4. Submissions can be sent by email or post. Remember to include your name, postal and email address and phone number, and indicate if you do not wish your name to be included with your story.

   Email: submissions@avocadopress.com. A plain text file or email body is preferred, but MS Word formats are fine too.

   Post: Send to Avocado Press, PO Box 22003, Khandallah, Wellington, New Zealand. Handwritten submissions are perfectly acceptable, but if you can type them, so much the better.

5. Posted submissions will not be returned unless a stamped self-addressed envelope is provided.
6. The writers of stories selected for publication will be notified prior to publication.
7. Stories are welcome from everybody, and given the charitable nature of our projects there will be no prize money awarded, just recognition for successful submissions.

8. The SPCA and Avocado Press have the right to publish extracts from the stories received without restriction of location or publication.

Have a look at the web site for ideas, sample stories and online entry: www.smarterthanjack.com.

Your details here:

Name: _____
Address: _____
City: _____
Telephone: _____
Email address: _____
Story title: _____

We'd like to hear your ideas

We would like to hear your ideas for future publications. What would you most like to read or write about? How could the books be improved?

Please complete the form below and post it to us at:

PO Box 22003, Khandallah, Wellington, New Zealand

or send us an email at ideas@avocadopress.com.

Your details here:

Name: _____

Address: _____

City: _____

Telephone: _____

Email address: _____

Your idea/s:

How to get more smart animal books

Would you like to order some more books in the *Smarter than Jack* series? Books available are *Smarter than Jack* (NZ edition), *Smarter than Jill* (NZ edition) and *Smarter than Jack* (Aus edition; available October 2003).

Postal orders:	Avocado Press PO Box 22003 Khandallah Wellington New Zealand
Telephone orders:	64-4-381 4470
Fax orders:	64-4-803 3347
Email orders:	orders@avocadopress.com

Your details here:

Name: _____
Address: _____
City: _____
Telephone: _____
Email address: _____
Titles requested: _____

Number of copies at $19.95 each: $ _____
Packaging and post per order in NZ: $ 4.00
Total: $ _____

Smarter than Jill

Delivery outside New Zealand: Write to or email Avocado Press to discuss payment and delivery options.

Payment options:
Cheque: please post with this order form.
Credit card: please complete the details below:

Card: Visa/MasterCard
Card number: ☐☐☐☐ ☐☐☐☐ ☐☐☐☐ ☐☐☐☐
Name on card: _____ Expiry date: ☐☐/☐☐

Thank you for your order. Please allow ten working days for delivery.

Here's something a bit different...

Bona Fide

53 True Kiwi Stories about Life as a Teen

Do you know a teenager? Do you think they find being a teen tough, exciting, lonely or just plain strange? Do they have good friends to confide in? Do they seem to keep their real feelings hidden in order to keep up appearances?

Well, *Bona Fide* is the perfect teen companion. It will give them a rare insight into what goes on inside other teens' heads. Chances are, they'll find stories in it that they can really relate to.

This 170-page book is a collection of 53 true stories about life as a teen written by people from all over New Zealand. Many are teens now, others wrote of past experiences.

In these stories many people have been extremely honest and graphic, so much so in fact that some have requested their names be withheld.

Project K will receive half the profit from sales of *Bona Fide*. Project K is a non-profit organisation with the objective of helping teenagers maximise their potential.

What's in it?

There are stories about discovery, sadness, reflection, observation, surprise, adventure, adversity, love, relationships, courage and motivation. Most end in a good way – for obvious reasons we've had to be quite careful about the message that the book sends!

The stories average around 800 to 1,000 words in length. A range of cartoons will grace the start of each chapter.

Overleaf is a taste of what you'll read about:

'"Stay with us, we need you," the nurse said, as I battled to stay awake. Then total amazement, when they dropped a skinny, pink, mucusy shape onto my stomach and I asked naively, "is that a real baby?" They hardly noticed me though, they were too busy. I heard no crying and wondered if it was something they only did on TV.'

· · · ·

'I was captured in her eyes, emerald gems dazzling from the fluorescent light. Her features seemed so soft and delicate. I wanted to touch her face but was afraid of the fragility. She was shrouded in a sweet vanilla essence. All the words were frozen in my throat. We were both caught in the silence of passing time. "Hi . . ." As she spoke the words drifted like music. I was helpless in her divine presence, feeling a wildly wicked sensation I had never felt before. Butterflies fluttered free inside my stomach, blood rushed like rapids, my heart thudded at a gallop. Love had awoken from a cold winter's hibernation.'

· · · ·

'I couldn't cry at all to start with, somehow I could still hear him laughing at me and calling me a short, girl, Nazi. I was so angry at him for getting killed because we didn't have enough time to make up our argument, like we always had done in the past. How dare he die before I could apologise for being so mean and nasty. How Dare He.'

· · · ·

'Making an entrance as a teenager is as important as planning what clothes to wear out. Not wanting to conform to the standards of those that lead sedentary lives, we decided to arrive at 10.30 pm. Early by standards these days! We all walked into the hall wearing our group identification: black jeans, boots and shirts with the name of famous bands across our chests. We carried our obligatory bottles in our hands and made our way to where those that were slightly older and supposedly wiser were enjoying the evening.'

'For most teenagers School Certificate is a time when you just spend weeks worrying about your exams. I spent my time worrying about what I could eat without feeling guilty. My reward after each exam was a lollipop – somehow that seemed good because the sugar would stop me fainting.

At the end of that year's prize-giving my friends said I looked awful and that they had heard people calling me 'skeleton'. Instead of this making me realise how serious it had all become I took it as them saying I was even more of a failure and basically it fuelled my anger and sadness. Why would someone like me deserve food? I know now how hard it must have been for my friends and family to see me like that. It hurts me to think how much I shut them out. I was in my own lonely world.'

• • • •

'One night, I had been talking with a guy friend of mine on the internet – and he basically admitted that he would rather date a friend of his over me, because he would look better going out with her. "For publicity reasons," he said, ignoring that she is one of the most shallow and insubstantial people I've ever met, and that he has more in common with me.'

• • • •

'I sit here in my drab nicotine-stained prison cell, contemplating my navel and sucking hard on a ciggy. What should I tell you first, that I'm five months into a two-and-a-half-year prison sentence of rediscovery and bitch fights? That my heart is so torn, I'm tempted to take to it with needle and thread. Or that the hand that holds this pen is connected to an arm so scarred it tells its own story in jagged pink ridges and valleys.'

'The reality of being 16 and not been kissed before caused me to panic slightly as David seemed so experienced and slick. He certainly was attentive. Here was a chance to put into practice what I had observed in recent films I had seen: the art of kissing with slightly parted lips. The test was here. In one experienced movement David put his arm around me and drew me close to him. Here was my chance to make the most of this situation. I reciprocated by promptly sitting on his knee and draping my arms around his neck. I tilted my head to one side, parted my lips slightly, closed my eyes, and waited. For a split second, nothing happened. Where were those lips? I opened my eyes wide enough to note the amazement on David's face. It looked as if all his delights had come at once.'

. . . .

'Instead of being the most academically important years of my life 5th and 6th form were the years I struggled to fit into the social arena. I failed 6th form certificate. When the final day of my 7th form came I sat at prize-giving with a twinge of regret wondering, if I had used my full potential would that be me receiving the Dux? Now seven years later I am a single mother on the benefit still in the same town with no qualifications. I have worked at the same supermarket job for ten years and hate it. I have aspirations of being a teacher and plan to enrol in teacher training in 2004 and finally I will be able to realise my dream of furthering my education and having a career. I know it's not too late, but I wish I hadn't left it so long. The ironic thing about my situation is this, the popularity that I worked so hard to achieve for all those years means nothing now.'

. . . .

'An unexpected person appeared in my life, her name was Nicole. To me she was the most amazing person, she had blue eyes that you could just peer into and get lost in. When I was around her the hurting and fear disappeared. I felt like myself again. I don't know if she knows she made me feel this way, but she did. I am forever grateful for that. I ended up falling in love with her, it's an unspoken love. It's so hard to tell someone you love them, specially if they are the same sex.'

How to get *Bona Fide*

Just complete this form. *Bona Fide* is available after August 30, 2003. Please allow two weeks for delivery.

Postal orders: Avocado Press
 PO Box 22003
 Khandallah
 Wellington
 New Zealand

Telephone orders: 64-4-381 4470

Fax orders: 64-4-803 3347

Email orders: orders@avocadopress.com

Your details here:

Name: _____
Address: _____
City: _____
Telephone: _____
Email address: _____

Number of copies at $24.95 each: $ _____
Packaging and post per order in NZ: $ 4.00
Total: $ _____

Delivery outside New Zealand: Write to or email Avocado Press to discuss payment and delivery options.

Smarter than Jill

Payment options:
Cheque: please post with this order form.
Credit card: please complete the details below:

Card: Visa/MasterCard
Card number: ☐☐☐☐ ☐☐☐☐ ☐☐☐☐ ☐☐☐☐
Name on card: _____ Expiry date: ☐☐/☐☐

Thank you for your order.